The September 11
Syndrome

Other books by Harriet B. Braiker, Ph.D.

The Disease to Please: Curing the People-Pleasing Syndrome

*Lethal Lovers and Poisonous People: How to Protect Your Health From
Relationships That Make You Sick*

*Getting Up When You're Feeling Down: A Woman's Guide to Overcoming
and Preventing Depression*

*The Type E Woman: How to Overcome the Stress of Being Everything to
Everybody*

The September 11 Syndrome

Anxious Days
and
Sleepless Nights

Harriet B. Braiker, Ph.D.

McGraw-Hill
New York Chicago San Francisco Lisbon London
Madrid Mexico City Milan New Delhi
San Juan Seoul Singapore Sydney Toronto

Library of Congress Cataloging-in-Publication Data

Library of Congress Cataloging-in-Publication Data has been applied for.

McGraw-Hill

A Division of The McGraw·Hill Companies

1 2 3 4 5 6 7 8 9 0 DOC/DOC 0 9 8 7 6 5 4 3 2

ISBN 0-07-140077-X

This book was set in Fairfield by Patricia Wallenburg.

Printed and bound by R.R. Donnelley & Sons Company

 This book is printed on recycled, acid-free paper containing a minimum of 50% recycled de-inked paper.

This book is respectfully dedicated
to the innocent victims of September 11,
their families and loved ones;
to the police, fire, and medical emergency teams
who responded so courageously to the tragedy;
and to the men and women of the U.S. Armed Forces
who voluntarily put themselves in harm's way
to defend us and our way of life.
Truly, this is "the Home of the Brave."

The only thing we have to fear is fear itself.

—Franklin Delano Roosevelt

Contents

The September 11 Syndrome

Introduction:
Why This Book

I want you to know that I thought long and hard before finally deciding to write this book. For so long it seemed that any public mention of the events of September 11 were sacrosanct, only to be discussed by reporters, politicians, and military leaders. I am none of those, and the last thing I wanted was to be perceived as treading on holy ground or in any way diminishing the memory of the many people who perished that day.

I am a psychologist, and one of my jobs is to help people cope with the stress caused by all sorts of different life events. It is what I am trained to do and, in fact, what I have been doing as an author, a licensed clinical psychologist, and a management consultant in private practice for more than 25 years.

Many of my private patients (who were among the first to urge me to write this book) still report that they are having trouble coping with life since September 11—and most of my patients live on the West Coast, thousands of miles away from the terrorist attacks. The nation as a whole is having trouble coping. Coast to coast, people are reporting that they are suffering from troubling bouts of anxiety and depression related to the events of September 11 and its aftermath. A full three months after September 11, a staggering 85 percent of Americans polled said that they felt certain that another terrorist attack *would* happen—but they didn't know where, when, or how. They just felt sure that it would. And while that percentage may be lower by the time you read this book, it doesn't alter the fact that our country is waiting for the other shoe to drop.

For example, in February 2002 and again in March 2002, George Tenet, head of the CIA and the national intelligence community, announced that more attacks against the United States were likely. Speaking before the Senate Select Committee on Intelligence, Tenet explained that although the Al Qaeda terrorist network had been badly damaged, it had not been destroyed, and, in his estimation, it was still capable of carrying out more attacks.

When a plane bound for the Dominican Republic crashed in New York two months after September 11, the first instinctive fear was of another terrorist attack. Didn't *you* think so? Even after the National Transportation Safety Board declared it to have been an accident, did you perhaps entertain the fear that maybe the NTSB was wrong? Many people did.

When a passenger aboard a Paris-to-Miami American Airlines flight apparently tried to detonate his explosive-filled sneakers in mid-air on Christmas Eve 2001, the so-called shoe bomber was swiftly overcome by alert flight attendants and brave passengers; the plane was diverted to Boston, accompanied by armed Air Force fighter escorts. It was inspiring and comforting that passengers and crew did not hesitate to subdue that terrorist, but news reports of the incident had the effect of sending anxiety levels soaring once again. After all, here was "proof" that the terrorists had hardly given up.

On another American Airlines flight a strong-willed pilot apparently refused to allow a man of Middle Eastern extraction to board his plane—even though the man was a member of President Bush's Secret Service protective detail and reportedly identified himself as such.

People are jumpy and nervous. One reason for their unease is that people are resuming—or at least trying to resume—the outward appearance of a normal life. After all, everybody wants to get back to "normal"—don't you? And if "everybody" wants to get back to normal, many people feel it would be an unwelcome conversational intrusion for them to raise the subject of the emotional difficulties they're having dealing with the events of September 11 and its aftermath. Perhaps they feel that they shouldn't burden others with their feelings about events that happened awhile ago.

The result is that many people feel isolated, strange, and maybe even abnormal that they're the only ones still feeling the lingering effects of stress, anxiety, and depression. If this description fits you, please know and take comfort in the knowledge that you are not alone in your feelings. This book will help you understand why you are having these emotions and what you can do about it.

One of the purposes of this book is to explain, from a psychological perspective, how the events of September 11 produced symptoms of a collective *acute* stress reaction all *across* America. The impact obviously was greater if you were near Ground Zero or the other attack sites, but make no mistake: the collective acute stress reaction I am describing was, and is, a national phenomenon.

Moreover, the stress is far from ended. Months later, there are still palpable psychological effects. Like the smoldering ruins that lingered for so long at Ground Zero, the anxiety of the nation also smolders, just beneath the surface in many cases. It is still palpable and tangible and fueled by massive uncertainty.

People can—and do—point to images or face daily recollections of planes going into buildings. They remember media reports of deadly anthrax in seemingly benign mail envelopes, and all the other reports you know so well, and wonder if they will be next. These are not unfounded or unreasonable fears. They are based on a frightening reality. We've all seen the terrorism first-hand (well, on television anyway) over and over again. These reality-based fears give rationality and credibility to the anxiety, and further compound it, especially as people try not to burden others by discussing these fears and concerns.

Following the events of September 11, and continuing to this day, an intense sense of vulnerability and loss of control has taken hold. These troubling feelings may linger beneath the surface producing heightened anxiety at any time, stimulated by replayed news footage of the September 11 attacks or by current news events from the war on terrorism. These jolts cause the embers to reignite into a flame of heightened anxiety and from there into more serious feelings of stress, depression, anxiety, and loss—*the September 11 Syndrome*.

This book will use strong, descriptive language to help you understand the reasons for this widespread syndrome. I do this because I am committed here, as I am in private therapy sessions with my patients, to speaking openly, candidly, and directly about a problem and its causes. Only by doing so can you get beyond the problem and (hopefully) delve into solutions.

This book is about solutions—about learning to cope effectively and even to learn the psychological skills of thriving under conditions of stress—so that you can enjoy a sense of emotional well-being. The promise of this book is relief in seven steps.

You will learn specific coping skills to stop the disturbing visual images from September 11 that may now be playing over and over in your mind's eye, and to replace them with other visualizations more conducive to relaxation, security, and other positive emotional states. You will discover a powerful method called "Thought Stopping" to interrupt the intrusive negative thinking that only perpetuates and deepens feelings of stress and tension, depression, and helplessness. And you will find out how worry can be regulated and contained so as not to invade your waking thoughts throughout the day.

These techniques and many more will help you personalize your recovery by addressing your own specific fears and anxieties that may be hampering your ability to conduct your daily life routines with relative ease and comfort. Furthermore, the seven steps will show you how to counteract depression by engaging in certain prescribed activities.

Finally, as promised, this book will teach you how to go beyond coping to reach new and even better levels of emotional functioning than you may have known before the September 11 tragedies. By creating and enhancing the *comfort* zone of your home, strengthening your *connections* with other people, and finding and developing your personal *courage*, you will learn how to turn our collective emotional adversity into your own psychological victory.

We may have lost our innocence on September 11, as so many have said, but a loss of innocence does not correspondingly mean a loss of optimism. As individuals, and as a nation, we have plenty of reasons to be optimistic.

I sincerely hope that this book helps you to get a grip in these uncertain times so that you can successfully and optimistically navigate your own way through the New Normalcy in which we all now live … and that the book can help you do more than just adapt; it can help you to thrive.

CHAPTER 1

The New Normalcy:
Outside in the World,
Inside of Your Mind

T he fact is the world has not been the same since
September 11, 2001, and I am certainly not the
first person to tell you that. Every place you turn,
it seems someone is saying, "September 11 changed
things forever." And they are right, even if they can't pin-
point exactly why things have changed or how to adjust.

Suddenly, abruptly, and without any warning, the
world as we knew it was turned on its head. And months
later we are still having a hard time coming to terms with
what is widely called "the New Normalcy." But why are
we having so much difficulty coming to grips with it all?

We have all lived through upheaval before, but we usually have had time to prepare for it and adapt; not this time. Even the attack on Pearl Harbor, which is routinely cited as the last time the United States was so viciously attacked, was not totally without warning. Historians point out that in 1941 we knew war with Japan was a distinct possibility. The administration of Franklin Delano Roosevelt was trying to negotiate peace terms with representatives of Japan on the eve of December 7, and while the actual attack caught us by surprise, we knew that hostilities between our two nations were likely and imminent if the talks failed.

That severe damage was inflicted on our nation on December 7 was a failure of intelligence and preparedness; but there was warning. And it was an attack on a military target, after all. By definition, a military installation should always be in a state of readiness.

But no one was ready for what happened on September 11, 2001. On that brilliant Tuesday morning, four commercial jetliners set off from East Coast cities, filled to capacity with enough jet fuel to fly to their scheduled destinations in Los Angeles and San Francisco. Using innocuous-looking box cutters—that easily passed through airport security—as deadly weapons, 19 Islamic fundamentalists hijacked the planes and turned them into guided missiles of murder, suicide, and mass destruction.

In a stunningly coordinated display of precision planning that both mesmerized and horrified the world, the hijackers flew two of the planes into New York's World Trade Center towers, exploding the symbols of America's global trade and financial power, first into blazing infernos and later into lifeless rubbles. We cried as we stared in disbelief at workers jumping from the highest floors to certain death below rather than face the fires of hell that their once safe office environments had become.

Then, the world bore witness to America's finest—hundreds of police, firefighters, and other emergency workers—selflessly rushing into the towers to save lives, often at the ultimate cost of their own.

At the same time, as if struggling to awake from a nightmare that wouldn't end, we saw the wreckage of a third plane that crashed into the Pentagon, turning the symbol of America's military might into another explosive blaze of murder and suicide. Finally, in an act of unforgettable courage, a handful of passengers on yet a fourth jet, apparently wrested control of the plane, which was bound for somewhere in the Washington area— from a team of hijackers and crashed to their deaths in a deserted field in rural, western Pennsylvania.

As the world witnessed—live!—the first military-style attack on American soil since Pearl Harbor, 60 years earlier, the unthinkable was transformed into the unbearable: Unable to sustain the intense heat generated by the massive ignition of jet fuel, the towers ultimately collapsed in immense clouds of dust, debris, and destruction that spread throughout most of lower Manhattan and beyond.

When the dust cleared, the once-booming financial district of New York was a war zone; the Pentagon had suffered a gaping wound; and a field in Pennsylvania bore testimony to heroes.

As of this writing, the recovery effort at Ground Zero continues around the clock.

To date, approximately 3000 lives have been lost.

September 11 was horrifically different from previous acts of terrorism directed against America in many ways.

For what was attacked that day was not a military installation, it was our innocence, our way of life—our normalcy, outside in the world and inside of our minds.

So, is that why September 11 has been such a sea change for the national psyche? What is it about the terrorist attacks of September 11 that makes life so different now? After all, terrorism itself is not new. Consider some of the terrorist attacks on Americans in the recent past.

Terrorism Before September 11

The takeover of the U.S. embassy by terrorists in Iran in 1979 did not *directly* affect most of us at home. In effect, life in America went on without missing a beat. The same was true in 1983 in Lebanon, when the U.S. embassy and, six months later, the Marine Corps barracks were bombed. In all, more than 300 military personnel and civilians perished. Tragic? Heinous? Of course; all that and more. But did it affect your daily life? No, not unless you were a relative of one of the victims. And even more recently, when the U.S. embassies in Kenya and Tanzania were bombed by terrorists in 1998, despite a combined loss of 224 lives, we at home were not affected in any way that changed us or our behavior collectively. And how many of our lives and routines were altered when the USS *Cole* was brutally attacked during a refueling stop at Aden, Yemen, in October 2000? Despite the tragic loss of 17 Navy personnel at the hands of suicide bombers, we as a nation were relatively unaffected.

Why? What was different about all those instances compared to September 11? Was it because those earlier terrorist attacks happened on foreign soil? Is that what made the difference in our collective response, our national consciousness? That's certainly a part of the reason, but it's not a full explanation.

These other attacks could be rationalized in ways that allowed us to still feel "safe" at home. Yes, we told ourselves, the world can be a frightening place. But most Americans felt relatively immune on American soil. The danger was not in our backyard. Our fears about suicide bombers in the Middle East—ghastly, to be sure—was something we saw on the evening news or read about in the morning newspapers. It didn't directly affect us. We were untouchable, or so we thought.

Next, consider terrorism at home. We've experienced that too.

The World Trade Center itself was bombed in 1993, and six people died. In 1995, 168 innocent lives were lost in the Oklahoma City bombing. Those were isolated civilian targets on U.S. soil, but we weren't affected the same way *then* as we are now by the events of September 11.

Do you remember the so-called Millennium Bomber? Around December 1999, a terrorist (later identified as a member of the same Al Qaeda group involved in the September 11 attacks) was caught trying to enter the United States from Canada at a border crossing in Washington. He was carrying enough explosives to achieve his goal of bombing Los Angeles International Airport on New Year's Eve. Because he was caught, his plot didn't succeed. And because the plot didn't succeed, our lives and our daily activities were not altered, even though a foreign terrorist directly linked to the Al Qaeda network tried to penetrate our borders and carry out murder and mayhem on our shores.

In retrospect, shouldn't our antennae have been raised? I don't mean the antennae of our intelligence networks and our armed forces; I mean our *personal* antennae. Shouldn't we ordinary citizens have been more concerned, more on our toes, more vigilant? Why did anyone think that having thwarted one lone terrorist at a border crossing would be the end of it? Why were we ignoring all of the retrospectively plain signals that more attacks were coming? Many of us were naïve.

Terrorism After September 11

Whatever the reasons were for closing our eyes to the risks of terrorist threats previously, they are wide open now. And while that is preferable, it is also part of the reason for our anxiety. We are now waiting and waiting for the other shoe to drop, and when it eventually does it will just make us more edgy and nervous. This is not healthy.

Obviously, there are real and lasting changes in the outside world. The damaged section of the Pentagon is being reconstructed, but New York City will forever bear the scar of the attacks; the World Trade Center will almost certainly never be rebuilt in its former state. Everyone knows it, and it saddens us all.

Moreover, we are constantly reminded of the gaping hollow when we watch any of hundreds of past movies or television shows. Filmmakers call them "establishing shots"—those quick images of a city's landmarks that tell the viewers instantly where the action is about to take place: the Eiffel Tower, Big Ben, the Golden Gate Bridge, the White House, the World Trade Center. For 25 years, the World Trade Center towers were used as *the* establishing shot to let you know that the movie or TV program you were about to watch was taking place in New York, the "Big Apple." Millions and millions of feet of film and videotape burnish that image into our heads. What happens to all of those old movies and videotaped TV reruns? The most vivid reminder of the attacks is right there in front of us. We see the towers and are instantly reminded of what once was. It's a constant pain in our hearts that is caused by a physical change—a change in the external landscape.

However, my expertise is not in explaining the events of the outside world. I leave that to the journalists and military and political leaders. My expertise lies in the inner landscape: the mind. And it is, in my view, "the mind" that is causing real problems for many.

From a psychological perspective, it is not the events that affect us; it is our perception and interpretation of those events in our minds. Each of us interprets events in a way that says, "How does this affect *me*? How can *I* deal with this? How does this change *my* world?" And in large measure it is here, in the mind, that we set the September 11 attack apart from all others, and that is what makes life so different for so many of us.

Understanding What Is Different

This book is about understanding how and why the cataclysmic events of September 11 have fundamentally altered the way most Americans think, feel, and act. As a direct result of that day and the events that have followed in its enormous wake, our lives have changed.

Things that we used to take for granted were taken from us that day. What we now recognize as the luxury of doing simple things routinely and without a passing thought, like going to work or on a trip, was brutally ripped away. We are now forced to think about the risk of doing previously simple things, as we never had to before. And, in part, *this* is the change that we're having trouble coping with.

It is human nature to want to return to normal as quickly as possible. That is why the terrorist attacks on our foreign embassies or military targets did not affect us collectively. It is because we didn't *want* them to, not because of a lack of sympathy or caring; far from it. Concentration of our energies on those other attacks would have deterred us from a return to our normal lives.

Prior to September 11, most of us operated largely in a state of benign denial. Yes, of course, we knew in our minds that there were terrorists in the world, violent criminals, mentally unstable people driven to irrational acts of violence, and political extremists who used terror as a means of gaining attention for their causes. And yet, in spite of the accumulating evidence cited earlier, we still adopted an "It can't happen *here*" mentality. We were protected by two vast oceans, peaceful borders, the mightiest military in the world, and a well-funded, capable intelligence network that could and would keep great harm an ocean's length from our shores. That is how we thought.

In retrospect, we may call it naïveté, or even the innocence of a free people. Perhaps it was a blind trust in the government, our military, and our nation's intelligence community. Whatever the reason, the "It can't happen here" mindset worked the way most effective defense mechanisms do: most of the time it blocked our awareness or perception of imminent danger. It buffered our fears; it assuaged our anxieties.

But on September 11, our internal psychological defense mechanisms endured a shock just as earthshaking and cataclysmic in proportion as the collapse of the World Trade Center towers themselves. As thousands died that day in the collapse and disintegration of symbolic structures of American finance and military might, our collective naïveté, innocence, blind trust, and denial crumpled, too.

A Change in Mindset

What September 11 has changed in our minds is our perception of risk: We now *know* it can happen here. It did. It is no longer an academic (or even military) debate about "what-ifs." What was once virtually unimaginable is now indelibly etched in our minds.

Moreover, we watched it happen. We have seen again and again and again the images of planes flying into buildings, buildings collapsing, people jumping out of windows. Those images are seared onto our mind's eye.

You should not underestimate or minimize the impact of this horrific imagery as a prime reason for feeling anxious or unsteady in the world today. With the exception of the attack on Pearl Harbor, there are no "as it happened" film or videotapes showing any of the terrorist attacks we talked of earlier. And even the scarce Pearl Harbor footage is almost all old, black and white, "after" footage.

In all other cases, unless we were eyewitnesses, we have seen only the "before" and "after" photographs. Even in the Oklahoma City bombing of the Federal Building, we saw the smoldering wreckage minutes *after* the bomb exploded, but we never saw the actual explosion and collapse.

The World Trade Center collapse left precious little to the imagination. But what there is left to imagine is at least equally horrifying: the terror in the eyes of innocent airline passengers; flight attendants held hostage by terrorists wielding box cutters; passengers telephoning from their seats to say I love you or good-bye (sometimes to total strangers or voice mail machines); and 19 Middle-Eastern men, whose faces we have seen from photos, taking over four airplanes. We imagine pilots struggling as the terrorists wrest the controls and convert passenger planes into weapons of mass destruction; we also imagine—with a combination of pride and sadness, admiration and tears—the remarkable heroism of passengers on one flight who stormed the cockpit and crashed the plane into an empty field in Pennsylvania, saving the fourth plane from crashing into the Capitol or even the White House itself.

Naturally, for many who live in New York and Washington, D.C., images of destruction were firsthand, along with the sensory assault of smells and the heat of fires that burned until December 19. In the days, weeks, and months after September 11, New York residents and visitors have faced a barrage of daily sirens, funeral processions, and constant recovery work at Ground Zero. While the impact of these events is inversely related to distance from the site of attack, in our American village, where television and the Internet connect us all, we have all been attacked.

Terrorism *has* happened right here, where we live with our families and work alongside our coworkers. Moreover, the faces of evil aren't far away—they live among us, blend in with us, all the while seeking and planning our demise and destruction. In an open and diverse society such as ours, how can we ever be safe and secure again?

Why has September 11 had such a profound effect on our national psyche? In part it is because we can no longer tell ourselves with assuredness that we are safe, or that our children or parents are safe; we can only hope, pray, and try to avoid danger even though we can't know if or when or where it's coming from next.

The "next" was anthrax.

Just days after the horrific events of September 11, the anthrax attacks began. But the anthrax didn't come to us by terrorist conveyance; the attacks were delivered as benignly—and diabolically—as possible by our friendly neighborhood mail carriers.

We'd been warned about the threat of bio-terrorism for some time. More than a decade ago, during the Persian Gulf War, those who are paid to know these things talked about Iraq's stockpile of bio-terrorist weapons and the threat that its dictator represented. But most of us chose to believe that danger would be limited to the field of battle. This was more naïve thinking on our part.

Terrorists—especially suicide bombers—do not fight by any rules, let alone by what used to be called "the conventions of war." Bio-terrorism was now waiting for any of us in the mail ... any of us ... in America ... in our hometowns ... in our homes.

When anthrax-laden letters started cropping up in mail addressed to high-profile news commentators and political leaders, we naturally sought reassurances from experts and government leaders. They accommodated by telling us the initial anthrax attack was an isolated event; but then there were more. Next the experts told us that anthrax is entirely, 100 percent treatable, and, besides, the fatal kind—inhalant anthrax—is exceedingly rare, hard to contract, etc. But then postal workers died, struck down by "occupational hazard."

Next, two women who simply opened their mail died; one was an elderly woman who rarely ventured beyond the safety and security of her own home.

Were these women intentional targets? No. Apparently they were merely innocent bystanders whose mail was accidentally contaminated by anthrax contained in letters directed toward someone else.

These events heightened our sense of vulnerability further and, therefore, raised our anxiety too, since they were such random and capricious acts. Who's to say *we* couldn't or wouldn't be next? The fact that, as of this writing, we don't know for sure who was behind the anthrax attacks only adds to our uncertainty and sustains our anxiety.

After all, where do we get our mail? Most of us get our personal mail in our homes, where we used to feel safe. But the anthrax threat even invaded that space where our children play and where we retreat to seek domestic refuge from our stressful lives. Our offices, too, were no longer safe harbors.

Ingenious terrorists took the ordinary, the banal, and made it frightening and dangerous—things like getting on an airplane and opening the mail. And that's part of what is so terrifying. The ordinary can no longer be taken for granted. Just the regular routine of living is fraught with danger.

In the weeks and months following September 11, periodically, various trusted people such as the attorney general or the director of homeland security (just think about that title: *homeland security*) admonish us to remain on "high alert" because "there is credible evidence that another terrorist attack is likely." But they don't tell us what or where or when. To heighten our confusion, six months after September 11, the Office of Homeland Security issued a color-coded level of terror alert—a rainbow of angst—but failed to instruct us as to what we should do in the face of various colors. We are simultaneously told to stay vigilant, and to be aware, but to carry on with our "normal lives." Has anyone figured out how to do this? I can tell you that it simply isn't "normal" to remain on high psychological alert indefinitely.

We are all searching for concrete markers to define the New Normalcy. But that search, in turn, breeds further uncertainty. And uncertainty breeds anxiety. If the new outside normalcy had a definite shape—something we could get our arms around and say, "OK, now I understand that these are the new rules"—we could probably adapt more quickly and easily than we are. But what defines the New Normalcy appears to be only constantly shifting sands. This difficulty we are experiencing in finding a solid footing is contributing to our twin sense of vulnerability and anxiety.

We have adapted to external change before, many times. In the face of certain harsh realities we have obligingly altered our behavior for our own safety and to protect our cherished way of life.

You might be old enough to personally remember the innocent days of open and unrestricted air travel, without elaborate airport security. There were no metal detectors or baggage searches then. You got to the airport, walked across the tarmac and jumped onto your plane; no one challenged or delayed you or asked for two forms of photo identification or who packed your bags. Flying itself caused the only anxiety you may have experienced.

But beginning in the 1960s, air travelers were occasionally subjected to hijackers who wanted to divert a plane to Cuba or some other destination. For the most part, these hijackers meant to reroute planes and obtain media attention for their political causes; their goals did not include suicide or mass murder.

"Hijacking a plane to Cuba"—doesn't that phrase sound almost benign and innocent today?

As a result of these hijackings, metal detectors were installed in airports to check for guns and knives. The concept of air marshals was born and they traveled on certain flights. Today, these metal detectors at airports and elsewhere are a fact of life and they have been for decades. You may even find it hard to imagine life without metal detectors.

Because of the threat of hijackings so many years ago we willingly altered our collective behavior. We agreed to get to airports earlier, to allow our carry-on bags and ourselves to be screened and searched, and to empty our pockets and walk through metal detectors. Now, we not only accept it, we virtually demand it. Still, airport security was itself a kind of New Normalcy at one time. But once it was explained to us and we could get our arms around it, we adapted and went on with our lives. We believed that airport security measures were an effective and, therefore, acceptable trade-off to achieve prevention and/or deterrence of hijackings.

But in the post-September 11 world, our faith in the airport security process has been sorely undermined. Not only do we harbor serious, well-founded doubts about the efficacy of existing security measures and their inevitably flawed human component, we cannot yet get our collective mind around what adequate security will ultimately entail.

For example, we learned that Richard Reid, the Christmas shoe bomber, went through security clearance at the Paris airport wearing tennis shoes ladened with plastic explosives. Now, we are told, all shoes must be screened. Although we are also told that only dogs or sophisticated sniffing devices, as yet unavailable to airports, can detect plastic explosives. Moreover, as of this writing, the majority of U.S. airports still lack the ability to effectively screen non-carry-on luggage for the presence of bombs.

Thus, when we don't yet know the extent of the adaptation we will need to make—nor totally trust the effectiveness of the procedures currently used—we cannot easily adapt as we have in the past.

The fact is that while we may have resumed many or most of the outward signs that life is normal and moving on, we nevertheless feel that our safety and security are largely beyond our control; whereas, a sense of control is what we badly need. Certainly, we feel we need to do *something*—that our government needs to take effective steps—proactively to gain more control, rather than just wait helplessly for another terrorist attack that may—or may not—ever occur.

In a metaphorical sense, we are collectively feeling our way in a darkened room after someone has moved the furniture. The old furniture is all still there, but it is just not where we remember it used to be; and there is new, unfamiliar furniture there as well. (In all of the other terrorist attacks before September 11, we never felt that someone was moving *our* furniture.) Now, getting from one side of the room to the other—a task that we used to accomplish day in, day out without even thinking about it—causes us anxiety, worry, and pain, as we bump up against things that weren't there yesterday.

In your mind, you know that if the sudden shifting of the furniture had some finality or closure to it, you could adapt. You could learn the new placements and adjust your meandering accordingly, even in the dark. You would be able to exercise some control over events. But what the nation is collectively experiencing is the realization that tomorrow night someone *may* move the furniture yet again, causing you to have to alter your behavior once more. Or much worse: maybe the whole house will blow up! And it is that uncertainty and lack of control that is causing much of our angst.

Naturally, there are limitations to the metaphor. For when merely furniture is out of place, the worst that likely happens is that you stub your toe or wind up with a black-and-blue mark on your shin. But, as we know too well, the real consequences of terrorism are death and destruction. My metaphor, therefore, is not intended to trivialize or dismiss the very real basis for your fears and anxieties.

But the metaphor *does* suggest what we all want back in our lives: safe routines and passages that we can accept and learn so that we can move on. We want to be more in control again. We want our interpretation of events to return our old sense of normalcy to us, or at least to define the parameters and topography of the New Normalcy.

We always knew there was risk crossing the living room in the dark, but it wasn't a risk we really thought about much. We knew we had to exercise a degree of caution—such as not running recklessly through the room when the lights were off—but the danger never prevented us from completing our task. When things were changed, we were willing to adjust our behavior in order to accomplish our excursion across the room with a minimum of risk, provided there was a "finality" to our behavior modification that allowed us to accept the new routine and stop worrying about it.

I cannot offer a return to the old normalcy; nor can I offer clarification of all the adaptations we may have to make to the new one. Nevertheless, I can reassure you that the current situation is in no way hopeless. On the contrary, this book *will* offer ways to regain a sense of control—concrete steps you can take to lower your fears and overcome your helplessness.

Remember, your sense of vulnerability to risk is a function of how prepared you feel to deal with it. So, by learning the coping and thriving skills laid out in this book, your level of preparedness for meeting the risk and handling the inevitable stress it entails will greatly increase. And, with that increased sense of control and security will come a *decrease* in your sense of vulnerability.

The fact remains, however, that a great deal has changed inside our heads and our minds since September 11. And, for most of us, those changes— while permanent or irreversible—certainly don't feel "finalized" yet.

Before September 11, we operated on a handful of basic assumptions, albeit naïve ones, about the relative risks of living as free Americans. Now, our old assumptions no longer serve us. Our old defense mechanisms no longer work to protect us against potentially debilitating anxiety, vulnerability, helplessness, and the depression that accompanies loss of control and confidence.

The unthinkable is now an image so indelibly frozen in our thoughts that it is almost as if it is imbedded in glacial ice, not likely to thaw or melt away anytime soon. We can conjure up the imagery in a millisecond—whether we want to or not. The images intrude on our conscious thought, invade the peace of our sleep, and transform our dreams into frightening nightmares. "[Seeing] a certain image at a certain time can take you straight back to that bright morning in September with the force of a body blow," wrote Holland Cotter in *The New York Times* some five months after the attack.

For the first time in many of our lives we perceive the world around us as a very dangerous place. Life has become risky. No one is truly safe, anywhere. "Evil" is no longer an abstract concept left to discussion by clergy or philosophers. Our president uses the word on a daily basis. There are "evildoers" in *our* world—our real world—not just in action comics or on old radio serials.

We know that terrorist attacks *will* happen again. We may have been naïve, but we're not stupid.

Perceiving Greater Risk

What has changed fundamentally inside our minds is *the perception of risk* we now associate with daily living. To better understand how you assess risk you need to know the two psychological components of that assessment:

The first component of risk perception is your appraisal of the likelihood that any given event might occur—in other words, the *probability* that a terrorist act or other dangerous event might happen. The second component is the degree of impact such an event would have with respect to loss of life, property, or disruption of the economy.

Before September 11, most of us believed that the likelihood that foreign terrorists could or would commit an act of terrorism on our shores—in our homeland— was possible, but not highly probable (we exercised denial—it won't happen here).

After September 11, most Americans (depending when they were polled) feel that such an event *will* occur to a certainty or near certainty—that another terrorist act *will* take place somewhere in America, sometime, somehow.

We witnessed the bombing of the World Trade Center by Islamic extremists in 1993. It was bad but certainly not catastrophic; we captured the "criminals" and "brought them to justice" in our courts. As a comparison point, the relative impact of the bombing of the Oklahoma City Federal Building by a domestic homegrown terrorist was far, far worse.

The cataclysmic impact of the terrorist act on September 11—combined with the planning, creativity, commitment, coordination, and evil intelligence that was behind it—was daunting. We can no longer underestimate or diminish these adversaries as bumbling or inept would-be bombers. They indeed have demonstrated a steely determination in long-term, careful planning and a shrewd intelligence.

So in the span of one bright September morning, our perception of risk went from minimal—not even on most of our psychological radar screens—to right in our faces, up close, and hideously personal. The images may still be with you when you close your eyes at night and trouble your thoughts when you awaken in the morning. In the aftermath of September 11, most of us felt overcome by a knee-wobbling sense of exposure and vulnerability. Psychologically, vulnerability increases—potentially to a paralyzing sense of helplessness and loss of control—when the degree of planning or preparation for risk is deemed to be inadequate.

As a country, we were woefully unprepared for this attack. As individuals, we were psychologically unprepared. Almost no one had a plan for how to deal with this sudden, intense sense of high-risk, imminent danger and these extreme levels of uncertainty.

Terrorism, by definition, strikes by surprise, without warning. The uncertainty of when, what, where is built into the very definition itself. Unlike conventional warfare, we don't see troop movements or armadas of ships sailing toward a new target. As mentioned before, our government leaders periodically underscore our vulnerability when they issue the "be vigilant/remain on high alert" warning, followed by the caveat that they have no idea for sure what's coming or where or when. Moreover, while we hope and pray those events don't materialize, our leaders run the risk of becoming the boy who cried wolf when the forewarned attacks don't occur. How do we know *anything* for sure?

This level of uncertainty not only breeds anxiety but creates levels of ambiguity that are uncomfortable for most people. We require more clarity; many of us are pleased when President Bush talks about "evil" because it's a black-and-white, clear-cut issue.

The events of September 11 changed something else within our minds: we now live with the palpable presence of fear. For most of us, our heightened sense of risk and uncertainty is not based on merely neurotic anxieties, phobic or irrational fears, or even generalized angst, but rather a very real and present danger. We all now live with a new *reality-based* perception of risk. We no longer can assure ourselves that we or our families are safe.

We are told to muster our courage just to carry on with our daily lives, let alone to attend sporting events and concerts, or to fly for business or just to go home for the holidays. Our fears are confirmed by the staggering amounts of money now spent on providing security—run by the Secret Service!—at our biggest crowd-drawing venues and at meetings of important political and economic leaders.

The "normal" we used to bank on is gone; living with risk and fear has become part of our New Normalcy.

The Challenge

Now we are challenged to develop new ways to respond, to make it possible for us to live as a free people, unconstrained by our own fears and anxieties, however well-founded and realistic they may be.

But the ever-present threat of terrorist attacks creates another problem that is well illustrated by a classic psychological study that demonstrates the impact of random negative events. The study involves a rat in a cage with electrified grids on the floor. Periodically, without warning, and unrelated to any particular behavior on the part of the rat, the animal is zapped with an electric shock. The rat has absolutely *no control* over whether or not it gets zapped. Sometimes everything is okay and nothing happens, and other times it's *zap, zap, zap*. Understandably, in no time the rat develops fear of the cage and the shock. It also develops high anxiety. Even when the rat is put in the cage but *not* given any shocks, the rat still remains so anxious it runs around squealing, in a state of fear, anxiety, and terror. It is the *anticipation* of the shock *and* the loss of control that are at work here.

Like the caged rat, we each need to come to grips with the electrified grid that America has become. If we don't get a grip, we'll end up feeling as unbearably anxious as the rat trapped in the "evil" cage.

We need a way to cope with the September 11 Syndrome—the anxiety, fear, depression, vulnerability, helplessness, trauma, sense of profound loss, anger, and outrage that lie just under the surface of our apparent resumed "normal" functioning. Indeed, we ought to find a way to do more than cope, to be even better—to discover our own personal courage so that individually and as a people, we can actually *thrive* psychologically—not just survive—in these uncertain and risky times. That is the hope and the purpose of this book.

We must learn to cope and to thrive because it seems there will be no finality on the terrorism front any time soon. President Bush has said that fighting terrorism will not stop when we capture and/or kill one particular terrorist. It is going to be a protracted fight, so we must dig in for the long haul. I find optimism and unity in that understanding, and I encourage you to do so also.

No one has said, "It's going to be *too long* a fight," or "It's a fight we can't win." By candidly acknowledging that it may be a long fight, we are also saying, "And we intend to stay in it until we win." Paraphrasing the President, the war on terrorism will end at a time and place of our choosing. I find optimism in that strong statement even as I, and others before me, acknowledge that the war on terrorism may never truly end in the conventional sense. A surrender will not be signed on the deck of a U.S. battleship.

Once before in our nation's history, a handful of madmen underestimated the fury of an aroused democracy. Our parents and grandparents—who have been called the Greatest Generation—rose to that challenge and defeated Hitler's Nazis, Mussolini's Fascists, and Hirohito's kamikazes during World War II.

Our nation quickly adapted to the then-New Normalcy of the war years and made sacrifices in the name of the war effort. We were united then, as we are united now, in a common cause to defeat a common threat to our lives and our lifestyles. Whether we stormed the beaches of Normandy or planted Victory gardens alongside the beaches of Atlantic City, we felt we were making a contribution to the overall war effort.

Accepting that we must adapt to a New Normalcy today—even one that has not yet been clearly defined—is a way of contributing to the war effort now. In this sense, my personal contribution to that effort is to share with you the seven steps of effective coping and thriving that will help you gain control over the troubling stress, anxiety, and depression that the New Normalcy evokes. This book will not stop with merely encouraging you to re-establish a sense of emotional balance in these uncertain times; it will show you how to do so.

I am optimistic that soon we will all begin to find our rhythm again. It may not be quite our old familiar rhythm, but it will be ours, and, hopefully, it will be even better and stronger.

CHAPTER 2

Here's What's Bothering You: Understanding the September 11 Syndrome

It would not be accurate to say that everyone has been affected the same way by the events of September 11 and the aftermath. To assert that would be to deny the unique backgrounds, personalities, and life histories—especially the exposure to previous trauma, coping skills, and circumstances of each individual—that determine how and why each of us responds to major crises the way we do.

In the first place, your relative proximity to the sites of the September 11 attacks will likely play a significant part in your reaction. To the extent that you were present and/or subsequently involved in the rescue and recovery efforts, or if you had a relationship to those whose lives were lost or to their families, you will be far more likely to suffer higher levels, more intense and farther-reaching symptoms of traumatic stress, anxiety, and depression than if you were farther away from the sites, did not know any of the victims personally, or never witnessed firsthand the sensory assault of noise, smells, sights, and movement associated with the attacks themselves.

Six weeks after September 11, a survey conducted by the New York City Department of Health of the mental and physical health of residents who lived near Ground Zero showed that about half of the people interviewed were experiencing physical symptoms, especially respiratory irritation in their noses, eyes, and throats, probably from exposure to the still-smoking fires from the World Trade Center ruins. Many of those surveyed also reported disruptions in their lives, and about 40 percent admitted to having one or more symptoms that have been linked to posttraumatic stress disorder: namely, sleeplessness, depression, anxiety, guilt, anger, irritability, and/or emotional numbness.

However, just because you were not actually at the scene personally or had no direct involvement with any of the victims or their families does not mean that you were protected or insulated from exposure to the trauma.

As you will soon see, even secondhand exposure via the media, Internet, or other means to the traumatic events of September 11 was sufficient to cause significant psychological stress reactions. In fact, the staggering proportion and horror of the attacks combined with their *live*, contemporaneous media coverage traumatized the nation as a whole, as well as individuals, in epidemic numbers.

For the first time, we witnessed terror *as it was happening*. We sat transfixed as we *watched* terrorists crash passenger jets into high-rise buildings, igniting their flying bombs with the explosive force of jet fuel in topped-off tanks. We *looked* at the carnage—at the multiple murders and the bold destruction of our cherished symbolic American buildings—as the attacks were taking place, *in real time*. We stared disbelievingly as the twin towers collapsed, burying our former innocence, naïveté, and security in their rubble.

We witnessed terror *as it was happening*, and then we saw the images over and over and over again.

In both positive and negative ways, our technology wove us together as never before. Searing heinous, horrific, and poignantly heroic images were broadcast onto our mind's eye. As a result, individuals from coast to coast, and all points in between, began to experience symptoms of *acute* stress—anxious days and sleepless nights.

The place you call home did not necessarily determine the immediacy or degree of your involvement on that September morning when terrorists struck our homeland. All too many West Coast residents were awaiting airline passengers or were passengers themselves when the three planes bound for Los Angeles and the one for San Francisco were hijacked and crashed.

The technological advances of our interconnected, wired world have nearly rendered moot the geographical distinctions and distances that kept us separated in an earlier time. Today, our very large American country has become a small neighborhood; and our larger world has shrunk to a global village.

For most of us, the trauma of September 11 was *virtually* experienced "up close and personal," almost as though we were right there in its horrific midst. The power of the trauma's impact on most of us who witnessed the events secondhand via television and/or computer screens is testimony to the technological intimacy we have achieved and accepted.

As a result, there has been a definite and, in many cases, profound psychological aftermath for *all* of us whose inner and outer worlds were changed by the cataclysm of September 11. When the World Trade Center towers collapsed, so did our previously inviolable sense of security and invulnerability, leaving us to struggle unprepared and unfamiliar with our own towering fears, anxiety, helplessness, and depression. No matter where we were on that fateful day, we all have had to tentatively pick our way through the emotional rubble, encountering the sharp edges of a new reality that is still taking shape in the post-September 11 world.

Why Define a "September 11 Syndrome"?

Few mental health professionals or other observers would dispute the contention that the events of September 11 have had an intense emotional impact on vast numbers of Americans—and others the world over. However, to date, the understandable focus of clinicians and public health officials, along with the corresponding media coverage, has been on detecting and treating the most severe reactions to the attacks: posttraumatic stress disorder, or PTSD. This focus is almost entirely confined to those *directly* impacted by the attacks—people who experienced *firsthand* the most immediate, extreme, and life-threatening trauma, including survivors, rescue and recovery workers, and their families and closest friends. It is important to note that even among those most immediately exposed to severe trauma, only a minority of those victims will actually develop full-blown symptoms of PTSD.

What about the rest of us who did not—thankfully—endure the most severe or direct personal exposure to the shock and trauma of September 11 and its aftermath? In all likelihood, we aren't vulnerable to PTSD. Can a meaningful pattern of symptoms—a September 11 Syndrome—be identified to help us recognize and understand the emotions we feel? Surely, we, too, are in need of help in order to regroup emotionally and regain our emotional balance.

In some respects, our very status as *indirect* victims compounds our problems. After all, don't our difficulties pale in comparison to those *truly* unfortunate souls—and their families—who lost their lives or were themselves directly traumatized by the actual attacks?

While appropriately humble, such invidious comparisons produce uncomfortable "survivor guilt" (e.g., "I have no right to complain") that lead to unproductive attempts to hide, cover up, or otherwise deny the validity or importance of our own feelings and problems. In effect, this survivor guilt has rendered us the "silent walking wounded."

It is important that a September 11 Syndrome be defined so that the emotional problems with which so many of us still struggle are recognized, validated, and treated. If not, the simmering anxiety, fear, and helplessness that still bubble just below the surface could well boil over into a serious, even epidemic, public mental health crisis and into even more serious emotional problems for you personally.

Once you (and so many others like you) recognize and identify with the September 11 Syndrome—a pattern of emotions, thoughts, and behavior that has developed in reaction to the traumatic events of September 11—you will find yourself empowered in several ways. Most important, you will be propelled onto a path of change and recovery.

Hopefully, you will take comfort in the recognition that you are neither alone nor "abnormal," strange, or otherwise maladjusted because you were—and remain—deeply affected emotionally by the events of September 11 and the aftermath. The feelings you have—the anxiety, fear, depression, helplessness, and loss of control—are essentially *normal* responses to an *abnormal*, disturbing set of circumstances.

A great many people who are otherwise high functioning and emotionally well balanced and well adjusted share these "normal" feelings with you. These emotional reactions are understandable and appropriate reactions to the heavy emotional burden that terrorism imposes on all of its victims and potential victims—and that includes all of us.

However, just because your fears and anxieties are to be expected doesn't mean that they are good for you or healthy to maintain over the long term. On the contrary, to passively accept and endure chronic stress and its companions—anxiety and depression—is to endanger both your physical and emotional health. In this critical way, the September 11 Syndrome provides a key target to guide your change and recovery efforts: When you know what's wrong, you can fix it.

Analyzing the syndrome will help you understand how the historical changes in our collective external reality have altered your private inner world as well. These effects, in turn, pose major challenges to your capacity to live with chronic uncertainty and increased vulnerability and risk.

Recognizing the September 11 Syndrome will give you an emotional vocabulary to describe what has been bothering you. With a common lexicon, you will find it far easier to share your thoughts and feelings with others and to benefit from the healing effects of communication. By disclosing your own feelings, you also will help others who may be reticent to talk about their emotional difficulties, either because they have lacked the right words or because they have felt embarrassed or ashamed to admit their ongoing emotional difficulties so many months after the attacks took place.

Finally—and this is my fervent hope—learning to cope with the September 11 Syndrome will help reduce the physical and psychological toll the attacks have taken on our country, our families, and on ourselves. Optimally, the techniques you will soon learn—the seven steps to help you rebound from anxiety and depression—will offer you the opportunity to live an even fuller and healthier life in spite of—or perhaps, *because* of—these risky and uncertain times we now must face together.

The September 11 Syndrome in Two Acts

The September 11 Syndrome is best described as a two-stage reaction. The first stage entails the psychological and emotional impact of the events on the day of their occurrence and in the days and weeks that followed. For our purposes, we will consider as "short term" those reactions that occurred during the eight-week period from September 11, 2001 through mid-November 2001.

The onset and actual duration of the short-term emotional impact will vary from individual to individual. As you will shortly learn, the nature of this short-term impact encompasses some or all of the features of what is clinically referred to as an acute stress disorder or, more broadly, an acute stress reaction.

For some individuals, the symptoms of *acute* stress appeared within the first day or two of the attacks and were likely resolved or remitted within the first two to four weeks of their onset. For others, the acute stress symptoms might have appeared somewhat later—say, within a week or two of September 11, but not later than four weeks after the initial trauma.

There is anecdotal evidence, for example, that people who found themselves in the midst of the immediate disaster relief did not feel the emotional assault of the events until several days later, when they were finally able to lower their adrenaline levels long enough to rest, think, and begin to process what had happened. Apparently, being in a state of high action somehow protected or prevented them from feeling the full impact of the attacks emotionally.

By definition, most or all of the symptoms of *acute* stress reactions develop within a few days to four weeks of the exposure to trauma; and the symptoms last anywhere from two days to four weeks from their onset. These parameters set the outside boundaries of an acute stress reaction at two months after the onset of symptoms or by mid-November 2001.

These guidelines follow the criteria set forth by the American Psychiatric Association and differentiate *acute* stress reactions from the longer-lasting and generally more debilitating effects of posttraumatic stress disorder.

The second, chronic or "long-term" stage of the September 11 Syndrome lies at the core of the problem today. After about mid-November—and certainly by the start of the New Year in January 2002—most of us had resumed, or gone through the motions of resuming, the activities and rhythms of our previously "normal" existence. In order to do so, of course, we have attempted to control our not yet extinguished fears by trying to keep them on as low a flame as possible.

But, despite our best efforts to get on with normal life, unimpeded by disruptive anxiety or debilitating depression, the disquieting features of the New Normalcy constantly confront us. Almost daily, we face the deeply unsettling threat of further terrorist attacks, as well as the loss of control over our ability to predict, prevent, or protect ourselves and our loved ones from the potentially cataclysmic consequences to our personal and collective security from such attacks.

As a result, a lingering anxiety and low-grade depression—the *chronic* symptoms of the September 11 Syndrome—still smolder. Because the New Normalcy continually exposes us to risk and uncertainty, the feelings we struggle to keep at a low flame periodically flare into disruptive, full-blown anxiety and even panic attacks that are fed by a deadening dread and sometimes a desperate sense of helplessness and loss of control.

The chronic stress keeps us on a hair-trigger emotional alarm system. All that is required to inflame our anxieties is a symbolic or actual reminder of the traumatic events. News footage, for example, of a light plane crashed into the side of a building in Tampa, Florida by a 15-year-old apparently "sympathetic" to Bin Laden's cause; reports of yet another Al Qaeda-trained terrorist trying to set his explosive-laden sneakers on fire with a match while crossing the Atlantic en route from Paris to Miami; or the sight of a crashed jet or fire in a high rise can all trip our personal panic alarms. Government warnings of "credible evidence of terrorist threats" or congressional testimony from the CIA Director that new and more severe attacks are impending easily arouse our barely latent fears.

The images of death and destruction are played relentlessly on our television screens at least every four weeks on the monthly anniversaries of September 11, and, not surprisingly, reappear as endless, alarming reruns in our mind's eye. At the six-months-after commemoration on March 11, 2002, CBS television aired a hard-hitting two-hour documentary that showed the attacks and collapse of the towers *as they happened* from the inside of the buildings. It's no wonder we are having a hard time putting the trauma behind us.

It is precisely the open-ended nature and constant repetitions of the September 11 trauma that make its emotional aftermath so difficult for us to contain. To better manage the emotional impact of that fateful morning in September, you must first understand in more depth how *acute* stress and trauma affect your ability to function psychologically.

Stage One: Acute Stress Reactions

Your initial exposures to the events of September 11—even if they were secondhand through television, news media, or the Internet—may have been sufficiently traumatic to cause symptoms of a clinical state called an acute stress disorder. As mentioned earlier, this is similar to, but shorter in duration and less severe than, the more widely known and publicized posttraumatic stress disorder. Many who were *directly* impacted by the events of September 11, unfortunately, are suffering from PTSD; but our focus here is on *acute* as opposed to posttraumatic stress.

What follows is a basic summary of the diagnostic criteria or symptoms of acute stress disorder as defined by the American Psychiatric Association. Unless you were present or directly impacted by the attacks, it is most likely that you will recognize or identify with *some* though not all of the symptoms. But, my purpose here is not to help you ascertain a definitive clinical diagnosis. Rather, it is to illustrate just how traumatizing the September 11 experience—direct or indirect—was for so many of us.

As you read through the list of reactions that follows, I believe you will realize that mere exposure to the horrific September 11 images was so stressful and traumatic as to make you and millions of others feel disoriented, detached, or deeply distraught. And why, even now, your mind is still working to interpret what these events mean about life, human beings, the nature of evil, and the prospects of safety and security in your own and your family's future. No wonder you've had anxious days and sleepless nights!

Here are the signs of acute stress disorder:

1. You were exposed to a traumatic event in which you experienced, witnessed, or were confronted with an event or events that involved actual or threatened death or serious injury, or a threat to the physical integrity of yourself or others. (In my view, watching the World Trade Center towers, even on television, attacked in *real time* and collapse qualifies as exposure to a traumatic event.)

2. Your response to the traumatic event involved intense fear, helplessness, or horror.

3. In addition to the above, you experienced *at least three* of the following emotions either during or after the traumatic event:

    ◆ You felt a subjective sense of numbing, detachment, an absence of emotional responsiveness, and distant or cut off from people.

    ◆ You had the experience of "being in a daze" and not always aware of your surroundings.

    ◆ While it was happening, or afterward, it seemed like things were unreal or like everything was a dream. This is called *derealization*.

    ◆ It seemed like your body, or some part of your body, was somehow changed, not real or detached from you; or you felt like you were watching yourself from outside your body. This is called *depersonalization* or an *out-of-body experience*.

◆ After the trauma, you may have had a brief blackout and may have forgotten some important aspect of the event. This is called *dissociative amnesia*.

4. The traumatic event is persistently re-experienced in at least one of the following ways: recurrent images, thoughts, dreams, illusions, flashback episodes, a sense of reliving the experience, or distress on exposure to reminders of the traumatic event.

   This would be true if memories about the trauma bothered you, or you saw images or had dreams, or you had moments when you felt as though the event were happening again—even though it wasn't.

5. Assess the severity of your symptoms:

   ◆ Do things that remind you of the event, including anniversaries of the event, get you upset? Do reminders of the trauma make you tremble, break out into a sweat, hyperventilate, or cause your heart to race?

   ◆ Do you consciously try to block out thoughts or feelings related to the trauma? Do you avoid talking about it?

   ◆ Do you try to avoid activities, situations, or places that remind you of the trauma? Or do you even try to avoid people that remind you of it?

- ◆ Since September 11:

    - ◇ Have you had problems sleeping?

    - ◇ Have you been more irritable or lost your temper more easily?

    - ◇ Have you had problems concentrating?

    - ◇ Have you been on the alert, always keeping your guard up with an eye out for possible trouble?

    - ◇ Have you been jumpy and easily startled by everyday, ordinary noises and movement?

    - ◇ Have you felt fidgety and restless?

- ◆ Have you experienced a significant impairment in your social, occupational, or other important areas of functioning? Has it affected your job, school, marriage, social life, and relationships with friends? Have you had difficulty, for example, telling others about the traumatic experience and how it has affected you? Did you feel extremely upset or distressed because of it? Has it kept you from completing your daily routine and chores—including traveling, flying, or going to public places or places where there are crowds?

Recall that the symptoms of an *acute* stress disorder last for a minimum of two days and a maximum of four weeks and occur within four weeks of the traumatic event. You can and should expect the acute stress symptoms to wind down within one or two months of the initial traumatic event. So, if these disturbances that reflect intense stress are still occurring today, and remain so disruptive as to impair your daily life, you may well be suffering from posttraumatic stress disorder or another serious emotional condition or illness and you should immediately seek the help of a mental health professional.

But what does it mean if most of your dramatic symptoms of acute stress have subsided while other, lower-grade but still troubling emotions persist? Should you expect *all* signs of fear, loss of control, or sense of helplessness to disappear or abate? If they haven't, what is it that is bothering you now?

Stage Two: Chronic Stress and the September 11 Syndrome

As I have repeatedly asserted—and it bears repetition again— after September 11, a great many Americans and others the world over are very much *still* affected by the long-lasting, lingering impact of *chronic* stress. It is notable, though not surprising, that within the first few months following September 11 there was a dramatic increase in the number of new prescriptions for antianxiety, antidepressant, and sleeping medications. There was also a spiked increase in the amount of drinking—alcohol being society's number one self-administered medication, although certainly not a recommended one, for nervousness, tension, blue moods, and depression. And, I am aware of no indications that these trends are declining.

So, what happened to you after the effects of acute stress and trauma subsided? Did all the troubling feelings you experienced wear off and just go away? By now, you know that they haven't—in fact, far from it.

What does remain is the essence of the September 11 Syndrome—a *chronic* stress response with two core symptom groups: (1) a pervasive sense of tension, worry, fear, and anxiety; (2) a pervasive, low-grade depression, sense of helplessness, and loss of control.

Let's take a closer look at both of these core sets of symptoms in order to understand what you may be feeling personally and to examine what might well be developing into America's newest emotional challenge of epidemic proportion. The first symptom is **a pervasive sense of tension, worry, fear, and anxiety**. Stress is a psychological reaction to change. In the last chapter, we discussed the critical *changes* in perception and interpretation of our New Normalcy and the psychological consequences those changes have spawned. Subjectively, stress feels like pressure. Most of us understand the expression, "I'm under a lot of stress," to mean subjective feelings of pressure, tension, and internal discomfiture or unrest.

Stress has clear physical manifestations, too. Stress-related symptoms run the gamut from headaches, stomach pains, backaches, skin problems, and an exacerbation or aggravation of just about every other illness or disorder you can think of, such as cardiovascular problems, arthritis, and diabetes. Stress can also lower your resistance and increase your vulnerability to a host of problems, including colds, flu, and other far more serious ailments.

Fear is an emotion that arises from the perception of danger. And fear typically has a specific target or object. For example, most of us feel fearful of terrorist attacks. We may fear invisible anthrax spores that could carry death in a benign-looking piece of mail. We may fear other bio-terrorist attacks. Or, much to our own chagrin and shame, many of us may now fear a particular group of people who, by virtue of their apparent ethnicity, bear a physical resemblance to the faces of terrorism that have been broadcast so frequently since September 11. In fact, people of all faiths—including Middle Eastern/Islamic groups—should fear the prejudices that have been aroused by the events of September 11.

But, when fear has no object or specific target—in other words, it is free-floating worry and tension not tethered to the perception of a clear and present danger, its name is *anxiety*. Uncertainty breeds anxiety. The pervasive, simmering anxiety to which many of us have grown accustomed since September 11 is fed on a nearly daily basis by the uncertainty of when, where, and how the next act of terrorism will be visited upon us.

Over time, that anxiety can create a sense of gloom and dread along with a generalized pessimism about life now and in the future. In turn, the nervous anticipation of "the other shoe dropping"—the dreaded next attack—drives more worry and a vicious cycle of anxiety and fear, helplessness, and depression.

Free-floating anxiety can easily attach itself to distressing recurrent thoughts. Anxiety feeds the obsessive worry pattern of what-ifs—What if this happens? What if that happens? Will my kids be safe? What would I do if my building were attacked? Should I even be working in a tall building? What if the airport security isn't secure? What if suicide bombers come to America and terrorize us as they have done in Israel? And there are many more what-ifs.

The potent combination of stress, fear, and anxiety can switch your body's regulatory system into a mode of constant alert, periodically escalating to alarm. The message from our government leaders is to remain *vigilant*—in a state of heightened awareness to signs of danger. But, staying vigilant overly long, particularly under conditions of high uncertainty, exacts a correspondingly high psychological and even physical price.

Your increased stress, fear, and anxiety since September 11 may:

◆ Produce fatigue and low energy

◆ Disrupt or interrupt sleep; increase disturbing dreams and nightmares

◆ Make you feel irritable and subjectively nervous

◆ Increase the amount and intensity of the time you spend worrying

◆ Make it more difficult for you to handle ambiguity, uncertainty, and decision making

◆ Interrupt your ability to concentrate or remember things

◆ Decrease your sense of trust in others

Your health can suffer from the ongoing effects of stress as described above. In addition, your health habits may become compromised by the increase in anxiety you feel—you may be drinking and smoking more, using medications or other drugs in attempts to calm down, sleep, or just stop feeling so jumpy.

Moreover, you may find yourself *avoiding* activities that you associate with increased feelings of anxiety such as: air travel; other forms of mass transport (e.g., trains or buses or avenues of transit, such as bridges and tunnels); sporting events, concerts, amusement parks, theaters, shopping malls, or other places where crowds of people gather.

When these avoidance behaviors compromise your lifestyle or your ability to conduct your daily occupation, responsibilities, or overall functioning, it is time to recognize the avoidance as a serious problem itself.

It is not difficult to understand how just the *threat* of looming terrorism creates chronic stress, fear, and anxiety. Recall, from the last chapter, the rat in the cage conditioned to unpredictable, random shocks. Even when the shock does *not* occur, the rat remains fearful (of shock) and anxious about just being in the cage and not knowing what *could* happen.

Terrorism, by definition, strikes at civilian populations (unprepared for danger) on an unpredictable, surprise basis. And, needless to say, the object of terrorism is to create fear, death, physical injury and mayhem, and destruction of property. Thus, the stage is set for all of us to feel like rats trapped helplessly in a cage not knowing when or where the next electric shock will come from.

Now let's examine the second core symptom group of the September 11 Syndrome:

The second symptom is **a pervasive, low-grade sense of depression, helplessness, and loss of control.** In the laboratory, a psychological subject (e.g., a white rat, a dog, or a human being) is exposed to an unpleasant stimulus—a loud noise, very bright light, moderate electric shock—on a random, unpredictable basis and in a situation from which there is no path of escape—no rhyme or reason, no method to prevent or control the "bad thing" from happening. The key words are *random*, *unpredictable*, and *futile*. The unpleasant stimulus is delivered on a random, unpredictable basis, thereby creating anxiety. In addition, the subject's actions are *futile* to control or prevent the unpleasant, negative consequences, thereby creating "learned helplessness." In clinical terms, learned helplessness goes by a different name: *depression*.

The September 11 attacks and the stress of the New Normalcy have created both the unpredictability and futility that combine to make low-grade depression an unwelcome presence for many people who have never before experienced moodiness or the periodic feelings of being "down, low, sad, or blue."

This low-grade depression is exactly that—low-grade, minor in key as opposed to major clinical depression, with its classic paralyzing sadness, inability to experience pleasure, loss of appetite, energy, concentration, enthusiasm, and, in worst cases, even the will to live.

The technical clinical term for low-grade depression is *dysthymia*, literally an "off," negative mood. Psychologists sometimes say that to dysthymics, unhappiness becomes a way of life. But don't minimize the toll low-grade depression can take because it isn't as dramatic or intense as major depressive illness. Just as a chronic low-grade fever saps your energy and vitality, low-grade depression has a corrosive effect on the overall quality of life and on your ability to enjoy it.

The aftermath of September 11 has left many of us sadder, muted in our enthusiasm and joy, always aware in the back or foreground of our minds of how slender is the thread with which we are all hanging onto life.

Low-grade depression may present itself in a number of ways:

- A heightened emotionality—weepiness, crying easily at nostalgic personal moments, sad movies, accounts of September 11 victims and their families.

- A sense of learned helplessness—a belief that there is nothing you can do to predict, prevent, or control the occurrence of a very bad event, such as another terrorist attack. Remember, when you believe that bad things can happen and that your actions are *futile* to stop or affect them, the stage is set for depression to step in.

- A heightened awareness of loss and/or its anticipation—finding yourself thinking about personal setbacks, "failures," and disappointments; and about the possibility of bad things happening to you or your loved ones in the future.

- A heightened sense of foreboding or propensity to predict and believe that bad things will happen to you and/or those close to you. This is called morbid or overly negative thinking. When you think that bad things *will* happen or are happening because you *feel* depressed or sad, you are engaging in a thinking error called *emotional reasoning*.

- A sense of loss of control—that you are less in control of your life, your future, and your ability to protect the people and things that matter the most to you.

- The sensation that there is a black cloud around you; a heavier weight on your shoulders when you wake up in the morning; a less enthusiastic attitude about your daily routine, work, obligations; less bounce in your step.

As you read these descriptions, you should know that these are understandable, basically rational responses to the events of September 11. The point again is that your responses are normal in the sense that many—maybe even most—Americans share them. But, *normal* does not necessarily mean desirable; nor does the fact that your feelings and reactions are understandable mean that they cannot or should not be changed.

The helplessness, loss of control, depression, emotionality, and sense of loss or fear of anticipated loss are real consequences of the fact that we *are* more vulnerable and more at risk of harm than we previously believed. And we now share the unwelcome knowledge that fanatics are capable of evil, maniacal acts that were previously beyond our capability to even imagine.

Now, who can listen to the news or read the newspapers on any regular basis without dreading the next piece of frightening or painful information that might be reported? Isn't this a reasonable and understandable effect of the cumulative stress that has built up in all our lives since September 11? Of course it is.

In fact, living with the September 11 Syndrome may be what everyone means when they refer to the New Normalcy and to the undisputed observation that everything and everyone has been changed since history's new date of infamy.

However, while you aren't able to predict terrorist attacks or know for sure where evildoers lurk, there *are* productive ways to handle the emotional aftermath of September 11 and beyond. This book is designed to do just that by:

- **Helping you to cope more effectively** with the real stressors, fears, anxieties, worries, sense of helplessness, loss of control, disturbing images, and depressing thoughts that the events of September 11 have created. By coping more effectively, you will be able to reverse the downward spiral of September 11 stress and rebound from its emotional toll.

- **Teaching you the secrets of psychological resilience** so that you can move beyond simply coping to levels of actually increasing your psychological well-being.

This book is not intended merely to describe a syndrome of anxiety and depression. Its purpose is to teach you concrete, effective ways to get a grip in these uncertain and risky times. Through action, you can and will learn to rebound from fear and anxiety, to overcome depression and helplessness, and, ultimately, to personally triumph over terrorism.

The world has indeed changed and it's up to you how you choose to meet the New Normalcy. You can choose fear, anxiety, depression, and dread. Or, hopefully, you will meet it with confidence, action, personal courage, and a heightened awareness of the sweetness of life, the preciousness of time and of those people and values that you most cherish.

In the next chapter, we'll look at the concepts of psychological coping and thriving, and then move on to the seven steps that will help you overcome the September 11 Syndrome.

Distress, Coping,
and Thriving

Coping effectively with the September 11 Syndrome begins with taking an honest inventory of how you *actually* feel, and not by attempting to compare your reactions with what you're told you *should* be feeling.

By early 2002, the prevailing ethos in the popular press and among opinion leaders and political spokespeople was that we should be "moving on." The implication was that to still be affected in some way emotionally or psychologically by the direct and subsequent events of September 11 and their replay in your head was somehow to show a weakness, maybe even an unpatriotic response. In other words, many of us were led to

Distress, Coping, and Thriving   55

believe that by "moving on" we *should* be able to put this behind us and get on with our lives.

To be sure, we were also admonished to "never forget" the events of September 11. What no one seemed to address was the fact that reminders of September 11— even symbolic ones—might constantly restimulate or trigger the symptoms of anxiety and depression we were now told we *should* leave behind or no longer be feeling.

Trying to make your emotions comply with orders by pushing yourself—or letting others push you around— with "should" or "shouldn't" directives is a huge waste of time. Merely telling yourself that you "should move on" or that you "shouldn't still be afraid" is simply an exercise in futility. Not only does it fail to stop or control the unwanted feelings, it makes things worse by adding additional feelings of guilt and inadequacy to the problem: you wind up feeling guilty about still feeling guilty.

By now you know that it is normal and completely understandable to have lingering symptoms of depression and anxiety after September 11 and to feel these emotions stirred up and exacerbated when there are events that bear real similarities or that represent symbolic parallels to the original sources of trauma. In fact, you should worry if you *don't* have any of these feelings. So don't think the only way to "move on" is to hide or deny your real thoughts and emotions.

Incidentally, this book will be helpful to you even if your symptoms of anxiety, stress, or depression were present *before* the events of September 11. In fact, it is likely that if you suffered from symptoms of stress, anxiety, and depression before the September 11 trauma, you would be even more prone to negative emotional reactions and for a more prolonged duration afterward than if you had never before experienced any such symptoms. In this sense, your preexisting symptoms of stress, anxiety, and depression have likely "primed the pump," rendering you even more susceptible and reactive to the events of September 11.

Alternatively, your symptoms of stress, anxiety, and depression may have developed acutely on or just after September 11 and may still linger at relatively low-grade levels. These may be novel or first-time experiences, or they may be recurrences of problems you believed you had conquered long ago. For those of you in the latter category, it is particularly important to realize that these reactions are normal.

What is most relevant to coping at this point is the fact that you have identifiable levels of psychological *distress* as manifested by anxiety, stress, or depression—not whether the origin of these feelings is directly related to September 11 or not.

Coping with Distress

Your psychological distress and emotional discomfort as a result of September 11 are *reality-based reactions*. Times *have* changed and your perception of the relative risk in living and the overall uncertainty and vulnerability that you—and all of us—face has been altered, probably permanently, since that morning.

But this does *not* mean that the appropriate response is to live in a state of protracted anxiety, fear, stress, and depression. In fact, doing so will exact a serious toll on your emotional and physical health.

In psychological terms, coping means that you are simply responding and adapting to the circumstances that you perceive. Often you are not able, nor do you attempt, to change the external situation or even your perception or interpretation of it. In this sense, coping is like playing the cards that have been dealt to you, the best way you can. Having little control over how you play your cards because you have little knowledge of, or experience with, the game can cause you to lose. This in turn can lead to low self-esteem and even greater anxiety and depression.

Coping *effectively* means you learn to respond or react in ways that produce less overall distress—fewer symptoms of anxiety, stress, fear, and depression as well as fewer signs of low self-esteem, which can come from feeling that you are not coping well. This book will assist you to cope more effectively by helping you more fully utilize the personal resources you currently have *and* by teaching you new skills, which will help you respond with less chronic distress to the New Normalcy.

But this book won't stop with just coping. The promise of this book is to help you to turn around your distress so that you can find ways to *thrive* and hopefully function even better psychologically than you did before September 11. At the individual's level of the struggle against terrorism, learning to thrive in these uncertain times is the ultimate personal victory. And, together, our joint personal victories make us a stronger collective—a triumphant American people.

Thriving in Uncertain Times

While negative stress certainly can make you vulnerable to illness—either physical or psychological—the relationship between the experience of stress and its effect on your health is more complex. Actually, what affects your health is not so much the level or degree of negative stress—or distress—itself, but rather (and this is key) *your perception* of whether the negative stress is essentially *out of your control* or, in worst cases, entirely *overwhelming*. Stress has the worst impact on your emotional and/or physical health when you feel powerless to filter or control its causes and helpless to change your reactions to it.

Contrary to popular belief, some stress actually can even be good for your health. This kind of "good stress" happens when we can interpret an experience as challenging, exciting, arousing, or fun or as one that gives life purpose and meaning. In fact, positive stressful experiences—meaning events that you interpret as positive or to which you discover or develop positive coping responses—can do the opposite of making you sick; they can have a lot to do with making and keeping you healthy.

Research has shown that the very same stressful experience can have toxic effects on one person while having neutral or even beneficial effects on another. One groundbreaking study, conducted on 200 top managers of the same company who were going through a stressful several-month period, found that half of the subjects developed signs of diagnosable illness—but the other half seemed unfazed by the stress or even better off as a result of it. Why? How?

The healthier executives in the study responded to and interpreted the stressful events in three fundamentally different ways from those who became ill. Their response style can teach us a lot—not only about effective coping but also about how we can learn to *thrive* under conditions of change, stress, and uncertainty.

Here is how the psychologically hardy subjects in the study—the ones whose health remained either unaffected or actually *improved* during the stressful period—reacted differently from the less hardy subjects whose health suffered as a result of the stress to which they were exposed.

First, those individuals who *thrived* under conditions of stress viewed the stressful changes to which they had to adapt as a *challenge*.

Second, the psychologically hardy individuals maintained a sense of *control* over the course of the stressful events that faced them. Instead of asking, "Why is this happening to me?" they asked, "Now that this has happened, what can I do about it?"

And, third, they exhibited a deep and abiding *commitment* to their work, families, religious beliefs, communities, and to other enduring values whose meaning kept them anchored while they rode the waves of stressful and uncertain times.

Subsequent studies with different groups all showed similar results. Those people who maintained good health during stressful periods interpreted the stressful changes in their lives as opportunities for *challenge* and personal growth; they had a greater sense of *control* over their lives and the stressful circumstances they faced; and they felt a greater *commitment* to the enduring values that defined their lives.

Thus, the hardy personality style has come to be known to psychologists as embodying the three lifesaving Cs: challenge, control, and commitment.

So to thrive under the present circumstances, first you need to respond by interpreting the situation as a challenging opportunity. Second, you must seek to find control whenever and wherever you can exercise it; but you must also let go of worrying about the things over which you have no or virtually no control. Finally, you must keep foremost in your mind your commitment to fundamental and enduring values that will persist throughout the stressful period and will be there when the period of acute stress ends.

As Americans, we have all seen a positive side to the September 11 tragedy. This is not to say in any way that the event itself was a good thing; it was a horrific outrage. However, as a people we became more united, specifically by joining in our collective renewal of *commitment* to the values that founded and still define our country. We have witnessed inspiring acts of courage and heroism of those who rose to the *challenge*. We have heard about airline passengers who exercised *control* over hijackers on Flight 93 that likely saved the Capitol or the White House from a direct attack, and, we have witnessed passengers and brave flight attendants take *control* and prevent a disaster when the shoe bomber attempted to ignite his explosive-laden sneakers on a transatlantic flight from Paris to Miami during the Christmas 2001 holidays.

Many of our leaders have exemplified psychological hardiness and the ability to thrive even during the most stressful of times. Who could watch Mayor Guiliani, President Bush, Defense Secretary Rumsfeld, and other government leaders in the weeks and months following September 11 without noting how these individuals seemed somehow transformed into their best selves as they fashioned active responses to the September 11 tragedy? They seemed energized rather than drained and depleted from the incredibly stressful circumstances they faced, as they rose to the challenge, exercised control, and renewed their commitment.

The Secrets of the New Psychological Hardiness

The events of September 11 and their aftermath have provided us with additional gifts—what I call the secrets of the New Psychological Hardiness. I want to teach you these secrets of the New Psychological Hardiness so that you can help yourself and those you love thrive as well as cope with the uncertainties and risks of our time. These secrets are embodied in the concepts of three additional Cs—*comfort, connection,* and *courage.* You will learn about them in Chapters 8, 9, and 10. They are the last three of the seven steps that will help you regain your balance in these unsettling days.

Look at it this way: If coping with stressful times means playing the hand that is dealt to you, as I mentioned before, then thriving means that you have the ability to change some of the cards for new ones. Think of it as the difference between playing stud poker (coping—playing the hand you were dealt) and draw poker (proactively exchanging some of your cards for others—taking steps to try to improve the hand you were dealt).

By taking an *active* stance against the uncertainties of our time and applying the techniques of the New Psychological Hardiness, you will discover your inner strength. You will be able not only to overcome fear, anxiety, and helplessness, but to actually feel more alive and to experience a heightened sense of well-being, even in light of the terrible events of September 11 and perhaps even because of them. You can become the kind of person who thrives by responding to stressful events in ways that actually benefit your overall well-being.

Here, then, on the pages that follow, are seven steps to help you get a grip in these uncertain times by:

1. Controlling the Images in Your Mind

2. Controlling Negative Thoughts

3. Overcoming Specific Fears and Anxieties

4. Overcoming Helplessness and Depression

5. Creating a Comfort Zone

6. Making Connections

7. Finding Your Personal Courage

CHAPTER 4

Step 1: Controlling the Images in Your Mind

The First Step in getting a grip is to learn to control and replace those disturbing images that have played and replayed in your mind's eye since September 11. As scary as the images were (and still are), you have the power to guide your thoughts in more positive, healthy directions. This chapter will show you how.

As discussed earlier but which must be reiterated, there are many ways in which the events of September 11 stand as unique in American, indeed, in world, history. The size, scope, surprise, and suddenness of the violence certainly marked our individual and collective psyches in ways that truly traumatized us. Moreover, most significantly, unlike other acts of terrorism, violence, and catastrophe before September 11, we *saw* the attacks and total destruction of the World Trade Center *as they happened*.

Think about this for a moment. While we have all "lived" through terrorist attacks before, most of us—and that means most of the world—have not actually *seen* terrorism before. We have seen only the aftermaths of terrorism. Even in the Middle East, most people who live there have never witnessed terrorism as it happens.

Most of us see the aftermath, the carnage, on the news ... *after* the terrorists' bloody acts are over.

Even so-called eyewitnesses to terrorism usually aren't. They may have been nearby or across the street or driving by. They may have heard an explosion, they may have spun around quickly, they may have been knocked to the ground, and they may have even been injured. But most of them didn't see it as it was happening.

Certainly, this was true of the Oklahoma City bombing. There were television news crews on the ground and in helicopters moments after the explosion—but that was *after* the explosion. We were horrified at the gaping hole that remained of the Alfred P. Murrah Federal Building, but we never saw the front of the building as it was being blown away, killing 168 people.

Those who may have actually seen a suicide bomber detonate himself or herself were probably *too* close and died in the explosion. And, while there may be isolated eyewitnesses who really saw a terrorist act, sometimes witnesses see different things. Or, in cases of severe trauma, witnesses may begin to question what they actually saw or their minds may banish the image from their consciousness as a defense mechanism.

There exists today some limited black-and-white film of the attack on Pearl Harbor, where a comparable number of people—approximately 2400—died on December 7, 1941, as perished on September 11, 2001. The film is terrible to watch, but even the first people who saw the film in December 1941 knew the outcome in advance of seeing the film.

The only thing I can think of that even remotely comes close to what we experienced on September 11 was the explosion of the Challenger space shuttle in 1986. It came close because many of us saw it live, as it actually happened; it was devastating to see it and know that seven lives had just been snuffed out. But it was an accident, after all, and what we saw was distant in the sky and not well-defined. We saw a fireball in the ethers, a vapor trail, but little else. The rest was in our imaginations.

But September 11 redefined horror and evil for the world. And it left precious little to the imagination.

We saw the planes flying into the buildings; we saw innocent people jump to their certain death from mind-boggling heights; we witnessed the incredible implosion and collapse of the towers, one at a time, and the subsequent demolishment of acres of Lower Manhattan that came to be called Ground Zero.

But, no matter where you lived in this country or elsewhere in the world, you saw the incredibly vivid and horrifying images on television. And the news media played them over and over and over again—for days, weeks, months.

Every day on the news—and almost every minute of every day on the all-news channels—you could see the smoke until it mercifully burned out in mid-December, and you could imagine the heat and the odors as the fires at Ground Zero continued to burn. As horrifying as the thought was, your mind had to know that here was the place where nearly 3000 people lost their lives. You knew that these were innocent civilians who merely went to their jobs that fateful morning and heroic firefighters, police, rescue workers, and other public servants who gave their own lives, rushing into the burning towers to try to save others.

Your mind has been assaulted with traumatic images. You witnessed the carnage as it was happening, and your mind filled in the horrifying details as the death toll mounted and the staggering reality of how few survivors were rescued from the burning rubble became appallingly clear.

Because these images were seared into your mind's eye and imprinted onto your brain with the force of trauma, you may still find those disturbing pictures with you even now, after much time has passed and most people have stopped talking openly about September 11 in their daily conversations. The upsetting images and thoughts may intrude suddenly during your waking hours for no apparent reason. Or they may just seem to reside in your mind's storage area, waiting for the slightest trigger to send them rushing back with alarming and unsettling speed and clarity.

You may think there's something wrong with you or unusual about the way you're thinking and feeling if you still are bothered by the intrusive thoughts and images of September 11 and its aftermath. Or you may be concerned that your periodic or even frequent preoccupation with "what if" thoughts of dangers and of yet unseen threats on the horizon may be signs of worri-some or dangerous psychological decline. You need to remember: These images are an entirely normal way for your mind to process what was, prior to September 11, virtually unimaginable.

Nobody Wants to Talk About It

Immediately after the attack, and for at least two or three months following, people still talked about their feelings, the images that plagued them, and the fears and anxieties related directly to September 11 and its aftermath. However, as time created psychological dis-tance from September 11, particularly since the bench-mark of the 2002 new year, psychologists note that for many, there appears to be what Roxane Cohen Silver, a professor of psychology and social behavior at the Uni-versity of California–Irvine, has called a "conspiracy of silence." Dr. Silver notes that everybody thinks that nobody wants to talk about September 11. But she adds, "If they aren't talking about it, it's not necessarily because they are not distressed."

Verbal and nonverbal signs of rejection may signal to you that other people are no longer willing to talk openly about the events or to hear about your fears or the pres-ence of those disturbing images in your head. They may say, "I don't want to hear about it," or they may use non-verbal signs such as appearing distracted or bored, or may merely shrug their shoulders and even walk away, Dr. Silver observes.

Silver, who is conducting a long-term follow-up study of the emotions of 1300 people in the aftermath of the September 11 attacks, reminds us that the inability to talk or the perception that there is a conspiracy of silence among your friends, family, or coworkers may have very harmful effects. In the silence, grief may fester and fears intensify. "The more others constrain your talking, the worse you get over time. We see an increase in distress over time," asserts Silver, as quoted in a *Los Angeles Times* story by Scott Martelle, on January 22, 2002.

The consequence of silence is your inability to engage in what psychologists call the *social comparison process*. This important process, in which talking and communicating allows you to place your own fears, anxieties, and other reactions in a context of how others feel, greatly aids in lowering anxiety by allowing you to "normalize" your own reactions. By hearing what you know to be true—that many others share your feelings, and the continued unwelcome presence of disturbing pictures in their heads—your concerns about the appropriateness of your emotional reactions would be largely allayed.

But when the opportunity to share these experiences with others shuts down, you are left to wonder how unusual your own reactions are. In that void, it is only normal to begin a process of reactive worry, anxiety, and criticism in response to your inner experiences. As a result, you become anxious and worried about *being* anxious and worried, and your problems are compounded.

On top of that, the concerns you may have are no doubt underscored by the constant drumbeat in the media to "move on and put September 11 behind you"—as if everyone other than you can just turn their emotions on and off like a faucet. Even if you could just "move on," how are you supposed to do that in the face of the distressing mixed messages issued periodically from our government officials that implore you to "be vigilant, remain on high alert, but resume your 'normal' life"? Just exactly how does anyone do that?

The truth is that you are emphatically *not* alone. The fact that the disturbing images of the attacks still appear unwanted and uninvited in your mind is quite normal and expected. And the presence of worry and disturbing thoughts is equally normal given the constant restimulation of images and threats since September 11 and the persistence of risk and uncertainty.

These recurring images are the result of living through a horrifying, violent event that traumatized you and that left you feeling intensely vulnerable. In addition, because it was caught live on tape, you have been subjected to it over and over again. These images exist in all of our minds. They can be easily triggered every time we find ourselves en route to the airport or even thinking about the possibility of boarding an airplane.

During the Christmas holidays in 2001—more than three months after the attacks—I remember a news broadcaster at LaGuardia Airport in New York interviewing a woman who had been waiting in line for several hours. She admitted openly to a live camera and open microphone that she could not get the vivid images of planes flying into the towers out of her head. And, she said, she just wasn't at all sure that she would actually be able to board the airplane once she finally reached the gate. This woman was willing to tell the newsperson what she could not or dared not verbalize to her fellow passengers. But there is little doubt that she was not the only one in line plagued by those images.

Having the belief that harboring negative thoughts and intrusive visual images is somehow a weakness or a sign of emotional inadequacy is simply incorrect and is likely causing you even more problems than not.

Criticizing yourself or ordering yourself around by telling yourself that you *should not* be thinking these thoughts or *should not* be seeing disturbing images compounds the problem further. Now you not only have the disturbing thoughts and images, but you are troubled by the self-criticism, guilt, shame, and other negative emotions because of your reaction to the fact that these thoughts and images still exist.

Both visual images and disturbing thoughts or ideas cause you distress; we know that. However, the reason that these thoughts and images have become a problem for you is not merely that they are there at all, but rather that they are not contained. That means that they disrupt your attempts to get to sleep as well as your waking thoughts. They interrupt and compromise your ability to concentrate. Intrusive thoughts and worries are a problem precisely *because they intrude* and interrupt your daily functioning.

The explanation for why you haven't spontaneously been able to rid yourself of these thoughts or control when and for how long they persist is that you haven't learned the best set of coping skills for gaining control over them. The first step, then, is to learn effective coping skills to control and replace the disturbing images when they intrude into your mind's eye.

Don't Fight the Thoughts and Images

You may have tried with all your might to ban the disturbing images of September 11 from your mind. When they occur, you may become angry or upset with yourself. And you may order yourself to "Stop thinking about planes flying into tall buildings, damn it!"

Unfortunately, as you have no doubt discovered, your mind has likely rebelled at this harsh instruction. As you have probably learned the hard way, your mind may actually fix on an image even more strongly when you admonish it not to do so. It's like the old joke about telling someone, "Now I want you *not* to think about a white polar bear sitting in the corner with a pink baseball cap on its head and a yellow and red polka dot scarf around its neck." With that kind of instruction, if you're like most people, you will be able to think of or visualize little else besides the humorously dressed polar bear.

So gaining control over the disturbing images requires you to acknowledge that the image is there. Understand that you are not alone and that you are not disturbed, deranged, or dysfunctional because the image reappears either with no apparent trigger or with an obvious stimulation or reminder—symbolic or real. Dr. Michael Schudson, professor of sociology and communications at the University of California–San Diego, calls this an "echo" of the initial attacks.

These echoes will be with us forever, so we had better learn to assimilate them into our everyday lives without letting them affect our ability to cope.

Remind yourself that you see and think disturbing things as a result of the September 11 trauma because you are a living, feeling human being who was deeply affected by witnessing a horrific event that your mind still needs to process and to try to come to terms with. The very fact that you can't easily assimilate these horrifying images as part of just another day in America is evidence of your emotional normalcy and your empathy.

If you could simply dismiss them or easily understand and assimilate the images into a preexisting category in your mind, you would certainly stand in the minority, and a worrisome minority at that. The overwhelming majority of people in America—and indeed around the globe—responded to the September 11 attacks as unimaginable horrors. When a horrible thing happens to one good person, it takes a long time for many of us to accept—let alone understand—the unfairness and sadness of the event. When that horrific and violent death is multiplied by nearly 3000, the absorption, acceptance, and processing can take a very long time, maybe even a lifetime.

So give yourself permission to see these images. You're not alone and you're not deeply disturbed if you continue to see the disturbing images.

But here's what you can *stop* doing: Don't engage in self-condemnation (What's wrong with me?) or self-criticism for having the images. Don't get stuck on the *Why* question—Why can't I stop seeing this? Why did this happen?

When you react critically to the presence of the image, you create a freeze-frame or a loop phenomenon in your brain's television screen. In other words, the image gets stuck there and you fixate on it as you engage in a futile monologue, telling yourself that you *shouldn't* be seeing this again or that you *must get rid* of these images.

What you have lacked until now is a program for what to do to effectively *stop* the image, to *change* the picture, and to *replace* it with images that conjure up feelings that are incompatible with psychological distress, anxiety, fear, and grief or depression.

By putting the techniques in this and subsequent chapters into practice, you will soon learn to corral and contain the distressing images and thoughts so that they stop causing distress by intruding on your waking hours. While no one can promise to control the content of your dreams, the technique below will also help you deal with distressing images that may awaken you from your sleep.

Get a Grip on Disturbing Images: See, Stop, Change, Replace

Here is an effective technique for dealing with intrusive images and flashbacks of September 11 and its aftermath.

First: See

See the image; don't fight it. Don't make it a polar bear with a pink cap and a polka-dot scarf. Accept and understand the reasons that your mind presents these images. They are evidence of the trauma, of your sensitivity as a moral, feeling, human being whose mind is having difficulty accepting, assimilating, and incorporating images that stand outside of the boundaries of what "could have happened in America" before September 11.

Allow the image to float through your mind. Don't fixate on it; just let it "be there."

Second: Stop

While the image is present, just *leave it alone*, but quickly shift your attention, as described in the following stop-sign visualization exercise.

Visualize a red, eight-sided traffic stop sign. You are standing about 10 feet from the sign. Be sure that you see the bright red color of the sign and can clearly read the white letters S-T-O-P on the red background. Follow the octagon shape around the perimeter, counting each side, from one to eight.

Now, visualize yourself taking 10 steps forward to approach the sign. Count off internally each step as you walk toward it. Notice that as you approach the sign, the clarity of the word *stop* begins to break apart. When you have completed the 10 steps, you are standing just a few inches from the sign. Notice that you can no longer make out the word *stop* or even the letters; note what the white against the red looks like so close up and how little of the whole word you can now see.

Now, back up 20 steps, again counting them off to yourself. As you walk backward, away from the sign, note how the letters again take their shape and contour on the red background; note how crisply the white letters form the word *stop* on the red sign. Notice also that the word is smaller when you are 20 feet away.

Now take 10 steps forward so that you are back to your original position. Look at the sign through the camera lens of your eye. Take the letters out of focus. When the letters are completely blurred, slowly bring them back into the sharpest focus possible. Note again the crisp edges of the white letters against the red background.

Finally, say aloud the letters—S-T-O-P—and then, finally, the word: *stop*.

If you can do this visualization exercise, you will effectively interrupt or stop the disturbing image that has intruded into your mind. This is because of one simple fact: Your mind cannot watch two screens at the same time. You can only visualize and concentrate on one image. So when the disturbing images intrude, use the stop-sign visualization exercise to gain control and to effectively stop the distressing images from rolling in on your mind's television screen.

Third: Change

Even though the images have been stopped with the powerful stop-sign exercise, you still need to take action to change and replace the image on your mind's television screen so that the distressing images can no longer be seen. You already know how to do this: Visualize yourself approaching the VCR/DVD control panel of your mind's television screen. See yourself pressing the Eject button and watch as the distressing image is ejected from your mind's VCR (or DVD) player. Just visualize yourself doing what you already know how to do and, in fact, do all the time: press that one big button on your mental VCR/DVD player that is marked Eject so that you can change the tape or disc. Say the words "Change this tape/disc" as you see yourself pressing the eject button. When the tape or disc is ejected, visualize your mental TV screen changing to a serene blue background. The words "Go on a Mind Excursion" are centered on the screen in dark blue letters. Say the words out loud or subvocally.

Fourth: Replace

The final phase is to take yourself on a personalized "mind excursion" that you will use to "replace" the disturbing images. To create this mind excursion, you will need to do a bit of preparation and you will need a tape recorder and microphone.

You will be developing three visualization scenarios, or what I call *mind excursions*. You need to write and then record three different types of "escapes." These narratives may be personal recollections or fantasies, but should adhere to the following outline of specific feelings:

The first should be a narrative or mind excursion of serenity, peacefulness, and calm. It should be a memory or an imagined scene that you associate with those particular feelings. Maybe you're walking in a garden or you're on a sailboat or out on a romantic date with your spouse or lover. It can be anything you desire because it is for you and you alone.

In the second narrative, try to be as free and carefree and creative as you can. Write a narrative that will enable you to feel exhilarated, revitalized, motivated, or euphoric. Perhaps you see yourself skiing fast at a favorite ski resort, or jumping horses, or water skiing. It may even be a sexual fantasy. As long as you feel pumped up by the description, anything goes.

For the third tape, think about things that make you feel safe and secure and comfortable. Maybe you're with your family in front of a roaring fireplace at the holidays, maybe you're snug in bed on a cold winter's morning. Perhaps you're on the beach at some real or imagined tropical island. Whatever your scenario, it is one that gives you a sense of reassurance and security and safety.

Finally, it is time to record each scenario in order. Remember, these are your personal mind excursions, so they should be written in the first person. The first one might begin, "I am sailing along in tropical waters. The sun is warm and soothing on my skin. The gentle breeze is enough to glide my boat through the calm waters."

The first and third excursions should be read into your tape recorder slowly, but the second—the one that is intended to exhilarate you—should be read at a faster pace.

When and How to Use Mind Excursions

Let's review: A negative, distressful image intrudes on your mind—images of planes flying into buildings, buildings collapsing, people jumping out of windows, etc.

Accept these as evidence of your normalcy and morality. Your mind is still trying to process the enormity of the evil, violence, and surprise of the events of September 11. For many people, these images have left deep wounds that are just now beginning to scar. The initial scars are likely to remain for life, though over time they will fade. However, any new attack, or even a threat of one, may reopen an old wound.

The very fact that these images reappear—whether you consciously understand the trigger or "echo" or not—are reflections of the trauma to which you were initially exposed and of the depth of your emotional reaction. The fact *does not*, however, indicate a weakness, pathology, illness, disorder, or problem in you or with your mind. Once you have accepted and acknowledged the presence of the distressing image, you will be ready to respond with the coping skills covered in this chapter.

The simple statement you will make to yourself is this: Stop this image. In time, the image *will* stop as soon as you begin the stop-sign exercise that you have just learned. With repetitive practice, you may not even have to go through the entire exercise. Just find the sharp image of the word *stop* and say: "Stop this image."

Next, you will visualize yourself ejecting the tape of the distressing images as described above. Say, "Change this tape/disc" as you visualize yourself ejecting the offending tape or disc from the player in your mind. See the blue screen and read the words *Go on a Mind Excursion*.

Create your own "menu" for your mind excursion with three options. You may title the narratives in any way that works for you, perhaps something like this:

Mind Excursion Menu

- ◆ Forest Glade
- ◆ The Rush
- ◆ Snug and Secure

Turn on the audiocassette player (the real one), close your eyes, and watch the screen in your mind's eye fill with the details of your personalized mind excursion. Because you have created scenarios based on your own personal psychology, needs, and experience, the feelings you select from the "menu" titles will naturally and readily be elicited as you allow your mind to travel in time and space to the scenes you have created.

Mental visualization—another word for mind excursion—is very powerful. Russian and Italian athletes, and others, train using visualization as well as actual activity. Research shows that visualizing yourself doing something creates muscle contractions, brain activity, etc., in your actual physiological response signs just as though you were actually engaged in the activity you are visualizing. Think about how "real" some dreams feel.

The point is that by gaining control and mastery of your mind, you will no longer feel like a helpless or passive victim subjected to the repeated horrors of distressing visual images of September 11 that play and replay in your mind.

Regulate Your Exposure to Distressing Images

Finally, if you have the television turned on and those images are being replayed for whatever reason, just turn the television off. If the newspaper or news magazine displays disturbing pictures, put it down. These images have already been deeply burned onto your mind's eye; you don't need to continually reexpose yourself if the images are disturbing. Maintain the mindset that the images are no longer going to control you or your mind; you will now resume control of them.

But there are other reasons to regulate disturbing images—your kids.

Now, while this book is about you—steps that *you* can take to overcome the September 11 Syndrome—I would be remiss if I didn't spend a few minutes discussing children and the powerful effect images can and do have on them.

It is not necessary to go into all of the chemical changes that are unleashed by the brain in the face of fear and anxiety and violence. Suffice it to say that these reactions are stronger in children. Danger and genuine fright can overload their small systems with adrenalin and biochemicals that may be hard for them to handle.

It can happen to anyone, but children are simply more susceptible to it.

The body recovers when the danger subsides. But psychological problems can arise when danger—in this case the same horrifying images from television and other news media outlets—is repeated over and over again.

"The shared emotion of a national tragedy can cause such medical problems even among those far from the scene of disaster," reported the *Los Angeles Times* in a December 23, 2001, story. "Television can reinforce the effect, said Kansas State University psychologist John P. Murray, who studies how the brain handles video images of violence," according to the article, by Robert Lee Hotz and Duke Helfand.

Because children's brains—as they are growing— have twice as many neurons and are twice as active and energetic as an adult's brain, prolonged exposure to violent images and real or perceived threatening situations can affect the growth patterns of young brains. This effect can consist of noticeable changes or it can be subtle. According to Dr. Bruce Perry of Houston's Child Trauma Academy, as quoted in the same *Los Angeles Times* article, "It can literally influence the way your brain organizes itself." No one is sure just how; every brain is unique, he added.

In short, if the images on television and in the news media are affecting you, just stop and think for a moment how they may be affecting your children. Also, keep in mind that children are excellent visualizers. If age-appropriate, teach your children the techniques you have just learned to empower them in the face of their own intrusive images.

In the next chapter, we will expand your newly acquired coping skills to manage disturbing thoughts and worries that were also created by the trauma of September 11 and its aftermath.

CHAPTER 5

Step 2: Controlling Negative Thoughts

Worry, rumination, obsessive negative thinking, and recurrent distressing thoughts are common symptoms of the anxiety and depression that are hallmarks of the September 11 Syndrome. In this chapter, you'll learn techniques for controlling your worrying—how to put your fears aside when you need to, and how to set aside "worry time" each day to acknowledge and effectively deal with your negative thoughts.

Since September 11, you may have found yourself spending more time out of each day worrying about personal problems and uncertainties specific to your own life. In other words, the *content* of your worry may not have changed, but you may be spending a greater percentage than usual of your waking time worrying, or perhaps the intensity or degree of tension and anxiety that are both cause and consequence of worry are greater than usual.

In addition, like many who suffer from the September 11 Syndrome, you may now find yourself burdened with a whole new category of worries. These are the "what if" fears that our newly acquired vulnerability to terrorism creates and the now more common "Should I or Shouldn't I" indecision that is created by fears and anxieties: Should I go on that trip? Should I get on a plane? Should I go to the football game? Should I drive through this tunnel or over this bridge? Should I go to a crowded shopping mall, or theater, or concert? What if terrorists target that place? These thoughts alone are sufficient triggers to full-blown anxiety and may even provoke panic attacks.

It's important to pause here to remind you that just because others in your circle of friends or coworkers aren't verbalizing their own anxieties driven by the September 11 Syndrome does not mean that they don't also share similar worries. Many of my patients report feeling better just knowing that they're not alone with what seems to be an overabundance of worry and negative thoughts that are continually intruding on their minds every day.

This chapter offers several simple techniques to enable you to stop and control negative thinking, obsessive worry, and distressing thoughts. We will begin by focusing on appropriate exercises for stopping negative thinking.

Thought-Stopping Techniques

The Stop Sign and Rubber Band Snap

In the last chapter, you learned a visual exercise focusing on a stop sign for controlling the *negative images* in your mind. The stop-sign visualization exercise can also be used very effectively to help interrupt, control, and ultimately stop *negative thoughts* from taking over your conscious thinking. As you have no doubt discovered, negative thinking can creep into nearly every corner of your consciousness, interrupting your ability to concentrate on work or other necessary or more pleasant mental activities. It's time to put a stop to that.

After you have become skilled at performing the stop-sign visualization exercise from the last chapter and can effectively stop and change a negative image by conjuring up a big red and white stop sign, it's time to add a wrinkle to that technique.

Put a rubber band on the wrist of your dominant hand. The next time you find yourself having a distressing thought or worry, and you are in a situation where it is possible to close your eyes for a minute or two and visualize the stop sign, snap the rubber band on your wrist sharply and say to yourself, "Stop this thought." Then, proceed with the full stop-sign visualization exercise.

The purpose of the rubber band is to condition the association of the snap on your wrist to the ability to stop a disturbing thought. Once you have successfully performed the thought-stopping exercise several times, the link between the rubber band snap and the stop sign will be firmly established in your mind. Then, you need only snap the rubber band when you find yourself having a disturbing thought and the snap itself will become a conditioned cue to interrupt the thought and to help stop it. Once conditioned, the rubber band snap can then be used by itself if you are driving a car or in a meeting or in another situation where it isn't possible to close your eyes and engage in the entire visual exercise.

To maintain the rubber band association and to keep your thought-stopping skill effective, be sure to do the full stop-sign visualization exercise at least once or twice a day, *immediately preceded* each time with a sharp rubber band snap to your wrist

Mental Distraction and Diversion

Another method for stopping negative thoughts is to focus your mind on an active mental task that is incompatible with the distressing thought you want to control. Your purpose is to apply the principle that your mind cannot focus simultaneously on a distressing thought and on a competing mental activity. Therefore, engaging in a different mental activity becomes an effective method of thought-stopping.

A number of mental diversionary techniques are incompatible with rumination, worry, and distressing negative thinking, whatever the specific content. Try putting your mind on solving a crossword puzzle, playing a computer game, or learning a new computer program. Balance your checkbook.

Try learning a foreign language by using audiotapes or a computer program. Audiotapes of books, self-help programs, or other instructional material are excellent for diverting your mental energy from intrusive thoughts.

Gourmet cooking from relatively complicated recipes is a good distraction. Hobbies that involve counting and concentration on patterns—such as knitting, needlepoint, sewing, model-building, ceramics, or woodworking—are examples of effective distraction activities.

Almost anything will work as long as it requires you to be mentally alert in order to work on the diversionary problem or task at hand.

The Geography Game

Another way to defeat distressing thoughts and worries is to engage your mind in a mental game or challenge that requires sufficient attention that you cannot simultaneously worry. One mental game that I have used quite successfully with patients troubled by obsessive thinking is the geography game. You may have played this game as a kid during a long car drive or bus trip, only now you will play the game alone.

Here is how the geography game works: You think of any geographical name—a country, a state, a river, an ocean, a continent, a city—any proper name of a geographical entity is acceptable. You must then think of another name using the last letter of the last entity named as the first letter of the next one. For example, if your first geographic name is Belgium, your next one must begin with the letter *M*—Mexico might be your choice. Then, the next name must begin with an *O*, perhaps for Oregon, and so on.

Engaging in the geography game when negative thoughts threaten to overwhelm you will effectively interrupt active worry and distressing negative thinking.

The Math Countdown

Like the geography game, the math countdown is another competing mental activity that will effectively stop and replace negative thinking because it requires concentration. Pick any odd number over 500. Then pick any odd number under 20 and count backward from the first number by the second. For example, you may select 697 as your number; and 9 as your second number. Your task is to count backwards from 697 by 9 to zero (or below). This activity actually works best if you're not a math whiz. The more you have to concentrate, the better the interference with negative thinking.

Acknowledging and Exploring Your Fears

The most distressing aspect of negative thinking and intrusive worry is the way they interfere with your concentration and completion of work and other constructive mental activity throughout the day. Although less disruptive, their intrusive presence while you are exercising, commuting, cooking, bathing, or conducting the other normal activities of daily life also contaminates the quality of the time spent doing activities that might otherwise be pleasurable or, at least, neutral.

In effect, worry and negative thinking disrupt concentration and other mental activity while they contaminate physical activity and activities of daily living. When worry and negative thinking get into bed with you at night, they make the otherwise very pleasant and relaxing process of falling off to sleep unpleasant, frustrating, and usually unsuccessful. Sleepless nights are an especially common by-product of negative thinking. That is because as you begin to close your eyes you are all alone with your negative thoughts.

The following activities are designed to help you control and contain your worries while simultaneously acknowledging and exploring them.

The Worry Box

To gain control over the intrusiveness of worry and negative thinking, you will need to regulate your worry time so that you can eventually reduce it.

To do this, you will need a small box or container of some kind to function as a "Worry Box." Any kind of container will do, but I recommend that you buy yourself a special little box for this purpose, and one with a lock is ideal.

Each time you have a worrisome or distressing thought that intrudes on your mind, jot down the content of the thought on a piece of paper. All you need is a quick note to help jog your memory later when you refer to it. After you jot the worry or thought down, put the piece of paper, folded up, inside the Worry Box.

When you put the note inside the box (or other container/envelope), tell yourself that you can't deal with it now because it isn't time to worry. You will now regulate your worry time so that you only intentionally engage in worrying or examining your negative, distressing thoughts during a period of no more than one hour (to begin with) that you will reserve as your "Worry Time." You can select any time of day that you designate as your worry time. The important thing is that you only permit yourself to consciously engage in worry and negative thinking *once per day*.

Understand what you are and are not doing. With the Worry Box, you are not allowing yourself to engage in a royal battle within your own head by trying to squelch negative thoughts. You are merely saying, "Okay, I'll deal with that thought—but just not now." That strategy alone should help you keep negative thoughts contained and under control until you are prepared to face them.

Then, during your assigned worry period, open your Worry Box and sort out your problems or negative thoughts into piles. Why piles? If you are a first-class worrier, you will very likely have several pieces of paper restating the same problem. Obsessive thinking, by definition, is redundant and repetitive. During your worry period, take out each piece of paper, read your note, and put the same or very similar thoughts into the same pile. When you have finished reviewing and sorting, throw away all but one piece of paper from each pile. You don't need all the repetitions to crowd your thinking—do you?

Now, during your assigned Worry Time, you can worry and review your negative thoughts. But instead of keeping all the worries inside of your head, you're going to write them down—uncensored—in a journal.

The Worry Journal

With a specially purchased journal or on a yellow legal pad, write the general problem, worry, thought, or concern from each pile at the top of a page. Then, let your mind stream on, one worry at a time. Write down the contents of your thinking. Try to let yourself just transcribe your thoughts onto paper, without editing or censoring.

You can decide how many different worries you want to deal with in a particular worry period. You can limit yourself to a selected number—try prioritizing by ranking the worries according to the amount of distress each causes you—and choose to "worry your way" through the most distressing thoughts first as they are likely to be the most intrusive and bothersome.

Or, you can divide your Worry Time (60 minutes total) by the number of worry piles, and write on each one for the designated time allowed. For example, if you have five piles, you can think and write about each for 10 minutes. (Remember to deduct some time for reading your notes and sorting them into piles. Sorting time counts as part of your overall allocated Worry Time.)

Don't write down the same thought in your journal more than three times. Worries are as obsessive, circular, and repetitive as broken records. To break the habit of obsessing, simply replace writing out a repetitive thought—once you have reached the limit of three times—with a big X mark on the page. Make an X mark for every recurrent, repetitive thought to indicate when you have had that same thought more than three times during one worry period.

Reducing Worrying Time

As you begin the process of worry regulation, one hour per day should be the outside limit for your Worry Time.

Regulating worry first involves corralling your intrusive thoughts and worries so that they don't interfere with your concentration and compromise the quality of your physical activities. You will do this by putting them in the Worry Box and restricting the time that you worry to the allocated Worry Time. However, regulating worry also involves *reducing the amount of time* that you spend worrying even during the allocated Worry Time.

You will soon find that one hour is probably too long for your Worry Time. This will happen as you automatically reduce repetitive thinking by becoming conscious of it and using Xs to replace redundant thoughts. And, over the course of even a few days, you will discover that you will tire of writing down the same problems or worries over and over again. This means that you are making progress.

When you decide that 60 minutes is too long a time to write in your Worry Journal, begin reducing your worry period by five minutes per day. You should try to start reducing your Worry Time by the second day if you can. Subtract five minutes from your Worry Time every day, every other day, or every three days, depending on your own sense of need to worry. When you find that you are running out of time to write down all your worries, that's okay. If you select a maximum of three of the most distressing thoughts that have crossed your mind each day, that is plenty for one worry period.

Your goal should be to limit your Worry Time to a maximum of 20 minutes per day or less. Many people find that 5 to 10 minutes per day is adequate. Almost all report that their anxiety and depression improve as the amount of time they spend worrying decreases.

Constructive Worry and Problem Solving

In truth, some worry can be constructive, if it is directed toward *problem solving* as opposed to repetitive, circular negative thinking. As you reduce the amount of time spent worrying, work on changing the substance or content of your journal writing from worry and uncensored repetitive negative thinking to constructive problem solving. Ask yourself for each negative thought or worry that you record in your journal, "Is there a problem here that I can solve? Is there something I can do to fix this concern or alleviate my worries?"

The key here is to sort out those things you have some control over from those over which you have no control. You then need to apply the rule that if you can't do anything about a particular problem or worry, there's really no point in spending a lot of time thinking about it.

Limit Exposure to Negative Thought Triggers: Turn Off the News

Many people who were deeply affected by September 11 and its aftermath became news junkies in the weeks and even months after the attacks. There is a compulsion to turn on the news to make sure that you haven't missed something "big" that might be happening.

But if you find yourself more upset, worried, depressed, and anxious after reading the newspaper or watching the news, it may be that you are overexposed to distressing information that serves to trigger and feed your worries and negative thinking.

Understand the principal difference between regular network news, for example, and 24-hour cable news shows. During times of crises or breaking news, the cable news shows glom onto the crisis *du jour* and broadcast it to death. Whether it's the O. J. Simpson trial, Whitewater, or terrorism, cable news shows are in the business of all news, all the time. So if you watch, say, MSNBC, you get a steady diet and constant drumbeat of the Big Story. The same stories repeated over and over again.

This is not to say that you should keep yourself in the dark or uninformed about the news of your community, the country, and the world. It is to say that spending *too* much time in front of CNN, MSNBC, Fox News and other 24-hour news outlets may be counterproductive to overcoming the psychological and emotional consequences of September 11. You need to find a healthy balance.

Allow yourself to watch perhaps one local and one national news show per eight-hour period. This would include a morning news show and an evening round-up of news. Watching continually won't give you any new information. It will just reexpose you to the same stories, many of which may be triggering unnecessary worry and distressing thoughts.

And, instead of watching reality-based news shows all the time, try substituting or mixing in some lighter fare such as situation comedies. A comedy might be just what your mind needs to relieve the negative thought cycle.

Bolstering Decision Making

One of the biggest problems that obsessive negative thinking and worry can cause is chronic indecisiveness. This happens most often when you feel highly ambivalent about whether or not to do something. For example, you may need to make a decision about whether or not to travel by air. When you reach the decision to go ahead and fly, you may then find yourself thinking about all the reasons that this may be a bad or dangerous idea. On the other hand, when you think you've reached the decision not to fly, you may then muster all the reasons why *not* flying is a bad or silly idea. In effect, you go back and forth, unable to make a stable decision because you use your obsessive thinking to talk yourself out of each decision you make.

This is analogous to buyer's remorse—the defective decision making of people who decide to buy something and then, by the time they arrive home, have talked themselves out of the purchase and feel compelled to return it. Then, after they return it, they may be tempted by the same reasons that they wanted to buy it in the first place.

The solution to unraveling your own decision making is to only permit yourself to strengthen or bolster your decisions by selectively focusing solely on reasons or arguments *that support the decision you make.*

There are any number of techniques to help you make a decision, from giving yourself a deadline, to assigning numerical scores or percentages to various options, to a listing of pros and cons. You should use whatever methods work best for you. Focus on the decision choice with the more favorable percentage. Write down all the reasons why this is the better decision. Don't allow yourself to focus on negative arguments against the decision you have chosen.

Effective decision makers utilize this process naturally. They reach a decision by evaluating information and their own feelings and by creating a decision deadline so that they are not plagued by ambivalence and the inability to decide. Indecision leaves you paralyzed, unable to move forward, and caught on the horns of your own defective decision-making process.

When effective decision makers make a choice, they bolster that choice by assembling all the reasons and arguments as to why it is the best thing to do. The benefits of this process are that you decide and *act* rather than become paralyzed by analysis paralysis. Applying this method will help you overcome the obsessive "what ifs" that create chronic indecision and self-doubt. Moreover, self-esteem is increased by effective decision making. Action—doing something active rather than merely obsessing—counters depression.

CHAPTER 6

Step 3: Overcoming Specific Fears and Anxieties

In the last chapter we talked about decision making. But what if your decision to do something is fraught with anxiety and fear? For example, many people developed an understandable fear of flying as a consequence of the September 11 trauma. This fear obviously has a basis in reality. Nevertheless, if your job depends on your ability and willingness to get on airplanes, being crippled by fear and anxiety to the point that you avoid flying altogether may endanger your employment. And that may be too high a price to pay to avoid feeling anxious.

After September 11, some people report difficulty going into high-rise buildings, which also may interfere with their ability to work or to conduct their daily lives. Even if they are not working in a high-rise building, their doctors, lawyers, or other people they have to visit might have offices in high-rises. Your fears may relate to driving over bridges or through tunnels or going into train stations or other places where there are crowds. Or, you may be avoiding concerts, sporting events, and other popular venues.

In this chapter, we'll discuss specific techniques for overcoming your fears and anxieties using the desensitization method. This step-by-step method will give you the tools and the confidence to take "counterphobic action" and actually shape and modify your behavior and reactions to stressors.

"Do Not Take Counsel of Your Fears"

It was U.S. Army General George S. Patton who advised, "Do not take counsel of your fears" when making decisions. It was excellent advice in battling the Nazis in World War II, and it is excellent advice in fighting terrorism today.

It is natural to have fears, but do not allow your fears to dictate how you live.

The techniques to control and corral worries and fears that we just covered will help, but you have got to make a conscious decision to not allow your natural fears to keep you from doing things that you need or want to do. And there are ways to do that.

Countering the helplessness of the September 11 Syndrome requires learning a coping skill to help you overcome your acquired anxieties and phobic fears. The powerful desensitization procedure I describe in this chapter is effective for gaining control over a specific fear or seemingly overwhelming anxiety that is currently preventing you from doing something that you need to resume doing. Your goal or purpose should be very clearly defined: For example, you may wish to overcome your newly acquired fear of getting on an airplane since September 11. Or you may wish to go shopping at a mall without feeling as uncomfortable or fearful as you now are. Any specific fear or focused anxiety can be tackled with this method, but you must first identify the goal of your efforts.

Try completing these sentences: I want to be less anxious or afraid of _____. I want to overcome my fears of _____ so that I can (do) _____.

Desensitizing Your Anxiety and Fear

The highly effective desensitization method is rooted in two basic principles. The first, like the use of distraction and competitive mental activities in the last chapter, is the premise that your mind cannot do two incompatible things at the same time. But now the two incompatible things are being anxious and being relaxed. Your mind—and you—cannot be anxious and relaxed at the same time. It's just not possible; you can be one or the other, but not both at the same time.

So, you will learn to substitute a relaxation response for your anxiety or fear reactions to specific activities, places, people, or other things that you now avoid or experience great distress approaching.

The second principle that forms the basis for this desensitization method involves visual imagery. For purposes of overcoming anxiety and fear, visual imagery can be used with great effectiveness.

Imagery, as you will soon learn, will be developed in stepwise, graded fashion. This means that if you wish to overcome your anxieties about flying, you will begin by breaking down the process of getting yourself to the airport and onto a plane into 10 small stages, from the least anxiety-producing to the most anxiety-producing.

The desensitization method consists of three parts. The first part involves learning a relaxation response by simply following the procedures for deep breathing and progressive muscle relaxation.

The second part is the creation of a list of 10 visual scenes that are ordered according to the anxiety caused by each image, from the least to the most anxiety.

The third part involves combining the relaxation and the guided imagery.

Learning Relaxation

To effectively desensitize your fears and anxieties, you will need to learn first what is called the *relaxation breath*; then you will perform the *progressive relaxation exercise*.

1. The Relaxation Breath. Don't you find it difficult, if not impossible, to relax when someone says, "Relax" or "Just relax"? *Trying* to relax on command sometimes makes a person even more tense than they were before. The relaxation breath is designed to relax you by having you concentrate on your breathing and not on your intention to relax.

Find a quiet spot where you can lie down and be comfortable for several minutes. Almost anything will do—

couch, hammock, floor, reclining chair. If you find soft music soothing, put some on. If you want to dim the lights or light scented candles, that is your choice, too. The idea is to create an atmosphere that you find conducive to relaxation.

The relaxation breath entails about three to five minutes of deep, rhythmic breathing. When you and the room are ready, close your eyes and begin to breathe deeply through your nose. Take slow, deep breaths of up to five seconds in duration. You should count to yourself slowly: one-one thousand, two-one thousand, three-one thousand, and so on. Try to hold each breath to a count of five and at the top of each breath, hold it for about one or two seconds before you slowly let it out for a count of five seconds.

You should repeat this for about five minutes. As you do the slow breathing, you should visualize waves slowly and rhythmically breaking on a shoreline. Try to visualize the wave in time with your breath—slowly lapping up on the shore for five seconds; then a brief pause before it slowly returns to the ocean, over and over again.

The relaxation will come; don't try to force it.

2. The Progressive Relaxation Exercise. Once you have mastered the rhythmic breathing by timing it to the image of waves, you will shift your focused concentration away from the waves and onto various portions of your body. This exercise works in tandem with the relaxation breath by having you progressively focus your concentration on different parts of your body in a systematic way while conjuring up sensations of heaviness and warmth. As you breathe deeply and rhythmically, you should begin to concentrate on a specific part of your body. I suggest starting with your right hand. So, either in a soft voice or to yourself, say the phrase "My right hand is growing heavy and warm." Then think about how your right hand is becoming heavy and warm.

After about 30 seconds, you will start to feel the effects, and you will have the sensation that your right hand has indeed grown heavy and warm. Once you have evoked that feeling in your right hand, you may switch your focus up to your right arm and repeat, "Now my right arm is growing heavy and warm." Wait until you detect sensations of heaviness and warmth in your right arm before you shift your focus once again. Next focus on your right shoulder; then, move gradually across your neck and head, and then over to your left shoulder. Continue progressively shifting your focus down your left arm and hand; then down the left side of your torso and down your left leg to your toes. Complete the circuit by focusing the sensations of heaviness and warmth over to your right foot, to your right leg, and finally up your right torso until you have completed the full body progression back to your right hand and arm where you began.

You will enjoy the deeply relaxing feeling of warmth and heaviness spreading throughout your body, from the top of your head to your fingers and toes. This exercise is designed to progressively relax your entire body, one part at a time.

Creating Graduated Stages

The next element in the desensitization method is crucial to effectively overcoming your fears and anxieties. You will need to create your own personal list of 10 graduated stages of approach toward your goal. Actually accomplishing the goal will be your tenth and final graduated stage.

For example, if your purpose is to overcome your fear and avoidance of flying, the tenth stage might be seeing yourself sitting on a plane with your seatbelt fastened and the flight attendant closing and bolting the doors. Or your tenth stage might be to see yourself in the actual takeoff of the plane or sitting in your seat during a long flight. Your tenth stage, by definition, should be the one that creates the greatest anxiety in you currently.

Stages one through nine must represent gradual increases in anxiety that parallel the stagewise approach to your ultimate goal. The first stage of the 10 should elicit the least anxiety. But you should still feel some degree of discomfort or low-grade anxiety when you imagine yourself carrying out the task you envision in stage one. In our example, the first stage might be finding out that you will need to fly somewhere for business. Or, it might be calling a travel agent or going on the Internet to book a flight.

The second of your graduated stages should involve a slightly greater degree of anxiety and so forth, with each stage increasing the amount or intensity of anxiety and fear that you experience if you think about actually doing the task or activity in mind.

The best way to construct your list is to identify your target goal first: That is your tenth stage. Then identify a first stage that creates a minimum level of anxiety relative to the goal. Next, identify the mid-range point, the fifth stage. What image can you envision that would elicit a mid-range anxiety response?

Here is an example of a graduated list of visual images created by one of my patients who overcame his fear of flying after September 11:

- ◆ **Stage 1**: Learning from my boss that I need to travel out of town to a business meeting.

- ◆ **Stage 2**: Arranging for the tickets with the corporate travel office.

- ◆ **Stage 3**: Packing for the trip.

- ◆ **Stage 4**: Saying good-bye to my family.

- ◆ **Stage 5**: Getting in the shuttle to the airport.

- ◆ **Graduated Stage 6**: Standing in a long line waiting to check my baggage.

- ◆ **Stage 7**: Going through the security check.

- ◆ **Stage 8**: Waiting in the gate area looking at fellow passengers; trying to be vigilant.

- ◆ **Stage 9**: Boarding the plane, getting into my seat, storing my carry-on bag, and fastening my seatbelt.

- ◆ **Stage 10**: Flight attendant shuts doors; engines turn on; taxi and ultimate takeoff.

Combining Relaxation with Graduated Images

Now we have arrived at the crux of the desensitization method. First, lie down in a relaxing position and perform the relaxation breath and the progressive relaxation that you learned previously. Do it at your pace and don't even try to do it "perfectly." Just let yourself breathe rhythmically and deeply.

After three to five minutes, you should be feeling fairly to very relaxed. At this point, imagine you are staring at a blank blue screen. Notice that you are able to remain very relaxed with the blue screen. Now imagine yourself in stage 1 on your list. See yourself as clearly as possible in the scene you have identified. Continue to breathe rhythmically and deeply and to keep your limbs heavy and warm.

As soon as you notice just the slightest degree of anxiety creeping in—which you inevitably will if your images are true anxiety producers—open your eyes and tell yourself to stop the image. Focus on a stop sign for a few seconds and return to the blue screen. Then repeat your relaxation breathing until you have resumed a relaxed state. Once again, envision the stage 1 image. Continue doing this until you are able to easily hold the first image in your mind for several minutes and remain relaxed while you do so.

Remember, your mind simply *cannot* be anxious and relaxed at the same time. It is impossible. Therefore, by pairing the relaxation breath and muscle relaxation response with your image, the anxiety response will be replaced by the relaxation response. When you have mastered stage 1 of your list of 10 stages, proceed to stage 2. Don't proceed to the next stage until you can successfully hold the images of earlier stages without becoming anxious.

Continue practicing your relaxation paired with the graduated stages approaching your goal. It may take several days or perhaps even weeks until you can successfully visualize all 10 incremental stages without feeling unbearably anxious. Every day, try to do the exercise once in the morning and again in the evening. Don't spend more than 15 minutes at each session. Go at your own speed or pace. Each time you begin a session, start with a blue screen and proceed through however many stages you have mastered—that is, proceed to visualize each formerly stressful image, noting that you now are able to do so without feeling anxious. In other words, don't skip anything; always start at stage 1.

When you have mastered all 10 stages, including your goal, you will be well on your way to overcoming your fear.

Counterphobic Action: Doing What You're Most Afraid Of

After you have completed the desensitization procedure using visualization, you will be ready to do what psychologists call *shaping the behavior* you have been most afraid of doing. This means approaching the feared goal in graduated fashion, just as you approached the visualized images.

Shaping the Goal

To do this, break down the actual behavioral goal into 10 actions, each of which is a graduated approach to the goal. The shaping will be most effective if your actual actions parallel your visualization stages. However, when you confront the reality of the goal you have feared, you may wish or need to change some of the stages by rearranging them or substituting new ones.

Countdown to the Goal

Ideally, you should give yourself at least one day to perform each action toward your goal. This means that you will need 10 days to conquer the fear that has paralyzed you or prevented you from taking a desired or necessary action. If your schedule does not permit 10 days, you may do the shaping in less time.

The important thing here is to understand once again that you cannot be anxious and relaxed at the same time. Because you will be engaged in actual behaviors, you won't have a chance to lie down and close your eyes to induce the full relaxation response. Instead, you will need to rely on the training you have done in relaxation breathing and signal your body's relaxation response by breathing deeply when you begin to feel anxious. Be careful not to breathe shallowly or to breathe too frequently. That may induce hyperventilation or a response that may make you feel dizzy and light-headed. Breathe slowly, rhythmically, and deeply to counter the effects of anxiety.

The basis of shaping relies on the fact that anxiety and fear will not persist in the absence of a reality-based danger. In other words, you can get over your anxiety if you force yourself to do the very thing you are most afraid of and notice that, in spite of your fears, nothing bad is happening *other than the fear itself*. So, the task at hand is to overcome your fear of your own fear and anxiety. If you run away or avoid the thing that scares you, you will merely reinforce the fear.

Millions of people have flown on planes safely since September 11. Many of those flyers had trepidation about getting on a plane after September 11. However, after they were able to face their fear and to see that nothing untoward happened, the next flight was far easier. And so it will be with you.

When you are doing each action of the shaping toward your goal, notice that you are able to overcome your anxiety because *nothing bad is happening other than feeling afraid*. Breathe deeply and notice your body relaxing. By taking yourself through each stage, from 1 to 10, in real life, you will be conquering your fear in manageable chunks. Your prior desensitization training will have prepared your mind to confront the possibility of anxiety and to replace the anxiety response with a relaxation response.

When you have completed the tenth action and achieved your goal, celebrate the fact that you have overcome a debilitating fear or anxiety. Consider this a personal triumph over terrorism. Remember, terrorists are effective when they make each of us afraid. By overcoming your fears, and resuming the activities and tasks of daily living, you are taking a personal stance against them.

CHAPTER 7

Step 4: Overcoming Helplessness and Depression

In the first few weeks following the September 11 attacks, the country collectively experienced shock, trauma, near-paralysis, feelings of profound helplessness, and an almost alien sense of extreme vulnerability to the propagators of terrorism and evil. We were pinned down in a psychological ambush.

By the second week following September 11, our government leaders were encouraging and urging us to get back to work, resume our daily lives, travel, and somehow rapidly adjust to the New Normalcy which, for most of us, hadn't yet even taken concrete form. While the advice was well-intended, think about how you normally mourn a tragic loss of a loved one. Isn't there a reasonable mourning period? Many of my patients complained that they didn't feel they had properly mourned the loss of life or their own sense of security and simply weren't yet ready to get back to "normal"; but they simultaneously reported feeling "guilty" because they were *trying* to return to normalcy. This sort of whipsaw thinking has contributed in no small measure to the September 11 Syndrome.

Although most of us—except for those thousands of families and close friends whose loss on September 11 was so profound as to alter everything in its wake—have by now resumed something akin to our normal daily lives, the lingering depression and anxiety of the September 11 Syndrome can still create the sensation that we are slowed down, drained of vital energy and optimism. We may feel as though there is a kind of drag in the water that, while not fully impairing our movement, has nevertheless taxed our reserves and made us feel that it just takes more out of us to live our lives each day.

Have you found, for example, that it is harder than previously just to get out of bed each day? For many people, the greater perceived risk in living every day under the imminent or vague threat of further terrorist attacks can create constant trepidation and can burden their mobility with the weight of chronic worry.

In order to overcome the lingering sense of helplessness and depression that lies at the core of the September 11 Syndrome, it is necessary for you to move away from the post-September 11 stance of paralysis, passivity, low activity, slowdown, and inaction to a more proactive stance. In this chapter, you'll learn simple, specific actions you can perform to make yourself feel better and more in control of your own life. These include such "behavioral antidepressants" as physical exercise, altruistic actions, laughter, and even a round of old-fashioned "spring" cleaning.

Change the Questions You Ask Yourself

All of us process new information by asking ourselves and others probing questions and by seeking answers to the questions. But, the questions themselves have important implications for whether we are able to meet uncertainty, stress, and risky times with a healthy active stance, or with one that becomes bogged down in analysis paralysis.

The cycle of helplessness and depression is fed by asking "Why" questions: Why did this happen? Why do they hate us? Why would anyone do anything so evil?

While the attacks of September 11 *directly* affected those who lived and worked in the World Trade Center and the Pentagon and those who boarded the ill-fated four planes that fateful morning, as well as their loved ones, the impact has in fact been much broader. The economic downslide that followed September 11, an exacerbation of a recession that had already taken hold on our economy months earlier, has had a profound effect on most Americans' lives.

The anthrax mail attacks made nearly everyone feel vulnerable in the sense that, at least theoretically, potentially fatal bacterial spores could find their way into *anyone's* home in the form of a seemingly benign piece of mail. Notable business benchmarks such as the collapse of Enron, the bankruptcies of Kmart and Global Crossing, and the downturn in the stock market broadly created disappearing acts out of people's life savings and pension plans.

So it's not surprising that these highly negative and apparently uncontrollable events led many people to ask why, why me, and what-if questions.

In order to overcome helplessness and heal depression, the why and what-if questions must be replaced by different questions. We need to ask ourselves:

- ◆ Now that this has happened to me, what can I do about it?

- ◆ Is there anything I can do to lower my personal risk?

- ◆ When I am vigilant, what should I be looking for?

Mobilizing yourself means asking yourself relevant questions, such as: Where can I go? Where do I want to go? What can I do? What do I want to do now? Who can I be? Who do I want to be? How should I act? How do I want to act?

These types of momentum-building questions motivate and propel us toward action, and action is the key to overcoming helplessness and depression.

Behavioral Antidepressants

What follows is a set of activities that I call *depression incompatible behaviors*, or DIBs. The rationale for using these behaviors to counteract depression is the incongruity principle, which means that a person cannot focus simultaneously on a distressing thought and a competing action or distraction, as discussed in previous chapters.

When your mood and your actions are not in sync or don't fit with one another, your mind will automatically correct the incompatibility by changing one to fit the other. So, if your behaviors are not compatible with the mood of depression, your mind will naturally set in motion a corrective drive to change your mood so that it becomes more compatible with your actions. You don't need to think about it; it will happen automatically.

So, using DIBs to treat your depression is like doing something natural, or "organic." By engaging in the set of activities described below, you will take advantage of your mind's natural tendency to rebound from a state of helplessness, blue mood, or depression in the presence of incongruous or incompatible behaviors. This is a prime example of your body fighting to take care of you, in spite of yourself.

DIBs can and do include a wide range of activities. The actions prescribed below are based on actual research that shows what people who are depressed tend to do—and not do—and, conversely, what people who are in positive moods tend to do and not do. So, by doing activities that are characteristic of positive moods, you will exert an *antidepressant* effect on your down or low mood.

There is, however, one key rule that you must apply in moving yourself from a state of relative inaction into action. That rule is that you must not wait to take action until you are "in the mood" or until you're "up for it"— that would be utterly self-defeating. The problem is precisely that you are *not* in the mood to do these activities in the first place because your motivation is depleted by depression.

The action rule requires that you *force* yourself to do these activities, whether you feel like it or not. By putting the behavior first—before your mood catches up with it—you will effectively leverage your mind's ability to change your mood and lift your spirits to come into line with the positive activity in which you are engaged.

Here are some of the depression-incompatible behaviors that will counteract and overcome helplessness, stress, and depression. Remember: Don't wait until you're in the right mood or frame of mind to do these activities. Do them in spite of the fact that you may not feel like it, and your mind—leveraged in the direction of a brighter and more positive emotional state—will follow.

Physical Exercise and Activity

The first line of defense against feelings of slumping mood and depression nibbling around your spirits should be to get up and move. Depressed people tend to stay very passive and inert. They lie around, stay in bed, sleep too much, become couch potatoes. Sound familiar?

Any kind of physical activity is incompatible with depression. The key is to *move* when you feel depressed. This can include walking, jogging, working out in a gym, swimming, bicycling, aerobics, dancing, jumping rope, and other solitary activities.

There is some evidence that timing moderate exercise about 20 to 30 minutes after a light meal can have a "thermic effect" on your metabolic rate, causing it to burn more efficiently. Many people report, for example, that doing moderate exercise (such as walking) after a meal creates an increased sense of well-being, more energy, reduced stress, and better weight control.

Sports obviously count as physical activity. Just make sure that the activity is enjoyable for you, not frustrating or overly, unpleasantly competitive.

Spend Time with Other People

Depressed people withdraw and think about their own problems; they become preoccupied with the why me and what-if questions. Being outgoing and genuinely interested in what others have to say is a potent antidepressant. Talk about your thoughts and feelings with others and encourage them to share with you. You may think you're the only one who still has residual or lingering issues since September 11, but you are *not* alone. While some people may not want to discuss the September 11 events and the aftermath, there are others who may welcome your initiation of the topic.

Do Charitable or Helpful Things for Other People

Depressed people avoid giving assistance to others or even being friendly. They tend to want to be alone when they are depressed.

In the weeks and months after September 11, a small army of volunteers converged around the Ground Zero site in New York to offer their services to the firefighters and rescue workers who labored around the clock to clear the site while preserving the dignity of the final resting place of nearly 3000 souls. Interviews with these volunteers, who were contributing their time and efforts to help, consistently showed that these people benefited emotionally; they spoke to the fact that they had a renewed sense of meaning, purpose, and community.

Other actions of New Yorkers—greeting the workers, cheering the police and firefighters—were other examples of how doing supportive things for others helped boost the mood and spirit of an entire city and indeed of an entire country.

Do Pleasurable Activities

When you are feeling low or depressed, your activities will tend to consist of a disproportionate number of things that you *have* to do but that are not particularly enjoyable, pleasant, or positive. This may be because you have limited energy and you feel as though you had better spend what energy you have on what you absolutely must do. People who suffer from blue moods don't have enough sources of pleasure in their lives.

Make a list of at least 20 pleasurable activities. Some of the items should require very little time, less than 15 minutes to accomplish. Other activities can take longer and require more planning. Add to your list regularly. Most important: Do at least two pleasurable activities every day.

Entertainment and Laughter

Get your mind off your negative thoughts by seeking out mentally engaging entertainment. Take yourself to some good movies; watch some good shows (not news shows) on television; go to a museum, concert, or music club. Listen to entertaining books on tape. And, above all, laugh. Turn on Comedy Central and watch old reruns of your favorite sitcoms; listen to comedy tapes in your car or on headphones. Combine entertainment with exercise—listen to good music or comedy or books on tape while you walk, bike, or work out.

Do you want to know if laughter really helps when you're feeling sad? Norman Cousins, the renowned former editor of *The Saturday Review*, first proclaimed the benefits of laughter in his well-known book, *Anatomy of an Illness*. He finished his distinguished career by acting as the ombudsman for patients—often cancer sufferers and other very seriously ill people—at the UCLA Medical Center, advocating the health benefits of laughter and positive mood states on recovery and pain tolerance.

Several years ago, the prestigious City of Hope Hospital, one of the nation's leading cancer hospitals, built the Cuervo Comedy Club on its sprawling campus so that patients and their families could find some laughs and comfort amidst otherwise hard realities.

Sweep the Floors, Sweep Your Mind

Believe it or not, cleaning your house or office when you are stressed can help improve your mood. Anything that you do that brings a sense of order out of chaos is psychologically therapeutic. If your home or desk can use a good cleaning now and then—whose couldn't?—now may be a good time for a spring cleaning, no matter the date or season.

I have given this advice many times before, to patients and to readers. Cleaning activities can enhance your sense of control by ordering what had been previously disorderly or chaotic. By being more organized you will know where things are, thereby eliminating the inherent stress that accompanies mad dashes throughout the house seeking misplaced items.

But I think that one of the benefits of these types of activities is that you don't have to think about them much. They require very little mental horsepower. So, during those times when you just don't have the energy for strenuous mental activity or you are otherwise feeling low, these organizational "no-brainers" will help divert your attention from the more stressful things on your mind.

I'm sure you won't have a problem coming up with a list of activities for organizing and cleaning your environment, but here are some suggestions that I've offered patients and readers in the past:

- Straightening up your home or office
- Washing/scrubbing floors, woodwork
- Vacuuming carpets
- Organizing your desk and drawers
- Reorganizing home or office files
- Cleaning out closets
- Sewing or mending articles of clothing
- Repairing broken objects
- Gardening
- Organizing tapes, records, CDs, books
- Updating address books or Rolodex files
- Refinishing or polishing furniture
- Getting rid of old magazines
- Organizing photo albums
- Washing and waxing your car

The Power of Collective Action

The days of passive passengers on airplanes are over. That ended September 11 when the heroes on Flight 93 taught all of us the value of collective action. When passenger Todd Beamer said "Let's roll," he was talking to and for all of us. When you heard about the passengers that subdued the shoe bomber, didn't it make you feel less helpless, and even proud that your fellow Americans, as well as the French passengers, were fighting back? When you get on a plane and look around you at your fellow passengers, you're looking at the power of collective action.

Sky marshals? Sure, we've got those and we'll get more. But in a sense, today virtually every seat on a plane is filled with a sky marshal—ordinary people who are not willing to be passive passengers in the face of terrorism ever again.

And let's not forget our men and women in the armed forces, taking the fight to terrorists where they live. When you listen to Defense Secretary Donald Rumsfeld giving regular briefings about how the Al Qaeda terrorist network is being rooted out of its caves, you may feel a thrill as you vicariously experience Todd Beamer's command, "Let's roll."

CHAPTER 8

Step 5: Creating a Comfort Zone

As a result of the events of September 11, many Americans have stopped to reevaluate their lives in light of the cataclysmic losses they endured or witnessed. This is understandable and, in fact, desirable.

Feeling vulnerable has made many of us turn toward the things that bring us the greatest sense of safety and security during these increasingly uncertain and risky times. In particular, we have invested more time and money making our homes more comfortable. And we are spending more time at home—video rentals are up, movie box office receipts are down. In the months after September 11, we spent money on home entertainment centers, DVD players, sofas, comforters, and other ways to "feather our nests" and to create a heightened sense of creature comfort at home. Even in the recessionary economy following September 11, Americans bought "comfort items" for their homes—candles, blankets, comfy furniture, and good books to read.

After September 11, Americans clearly started staying at home more than traveling; spending their money on ways to make their homes and apartments more comfortable, cozy, and safe; eating what some of us consider old-fashioned foods—macaroni and cheese, meatloaf, Campbell soups, and other comfort foods. There was a renewed interest in both preparing and eating home-cooked food as well as a surge in ready-to-eat food deliveries to homes. For millions of Americans, ordering out for a pizza and curling up on the couch to watch a great movie became infinitely more appealing—and felt far safer—than going out to dinner and a theater.

The trend is clearly toward a nesting phenomenon in our homes. We are trying to create greater comfort where we want to feel most secure—in our homes. To a very significant extent, we are closing out the world, staying home and cocooning.

With our increased sensitivity to the fragility of life, we are focusing more on our families and on the homes we make for ourselves. And when you stop to think about it, is that such a bad thing? Of course not.

Increasing your sense of safety and comfort at home is both an effective coping skill as well as one way in which you can *thrive*—that is, improve your psychological, emotional, and physical health—in the aftermath of September 11.

Turning back toward home and the comforts it provides is also a move toward renewed commitment: to our families, our way of life, our freedom, and our treasured but now violated sense of security.

Creating a comfort zone is in many respects analogous to creating a safety zone. Typically, the place where "danger lurks" is out there in the cold, harsh world. Home, though, has usually been considered a place of safety and refuge. When we come home and close the front door behind us, we feel a sense of safety by virtue of what we've left outside the door.

If we've had a harrowing car commute filled with heavy traffic, erratic drivers, honking horns, or even an accident or fender-bender, we feel intense relief to finally park the car and come into the safety of our houses or apartments, leaving the "madness" behind.

If we've had a hard day at work filled with demanding bosses and unreasonable coworkers, difficult clients or rude customers, flaring tempers, raised voices, and harsh reprimands, don't we count the hours and the minutes until it's quitting time and we can get home to unwind from the crazy day and the crazy-makers?

Going back to when we were little kids, home for most of us has ideally been a haven, a place of safety, or a safety zone. If we were lucky as children, it was almost always comforting and reassuring to come home to Mom and Dad, to feel their protective presence in their loving arms. Today, by creating comfort in our safety zones, we develop a psychological advantage over the bad guys.

There are, of course, limitations to the appropriateness of staying home. Clearly, this can go too far or last too long. But, as long as you are continuing with your work or job and maintaining the activities of your daily life, and you are not avoiding going outside your home because of phobic anxiety, the tendency to derive an enhanced sense of comfort and security by staying home is a healthy trend. This is especially true if it means spending more quality time with family and friends.

In the weeks and early months after September 11, officials of the government repeatedly convened the news media to announce that law enforcement across the nation, as well as every citizen, should be vigilant to the credible threat of a new terrorist attack. Nearly five months after the September 11 attack, Defense Secretary Donald Rumsfeld said the United States must prepare for potential surprise attacks "vastly more deadly" than the September 11 terrorist hijackings. And, at the six-month mark, as mentioned previously, Homeland Security Director Tom Ridge catapulted our anxiety into a new ambiguous spectrum of color-coded levels of alarm.

These frightening messages further increased our uncertainty and stress by failing to say with any specificity where, when, or what kind of attack might be imminent or what actual steps we should take to protect and defend ourselves should these "credible threats" materialize into an actual attack

We are told to remain "vigilant" and on "high alert" while being encouraged at the same time to resume our normal daily lives. But this advice—to remain vigilantly normal—is a confusing, and virtually impossible oxymoron.

Sustaining a state of heightened vigilance and high alert poses a potentially serious threat to health and can compromise overall quality of life. Overactivation of the stress-arousal system in our bodies can increase the risk of cardiovascular illnesses, including stroke, heart attack, and high blood pressure, and can lower immune functioning.

The fact is that you cannot remain in a state of high vigilance without becoming either chronically anxious, panicky, or just plain exhausted. Staying at home, at least some of the time, perhaps more often and for longer periods than before September 11, affords you the opportunity to "stand down"—be "at ease," in military parlance—from the increased vigilance.

Turning your home into a comfort zone is also a fine method of stress reduction. When you practice the relaxation breathing and progressive relaxation that we covered in Chapter 6 as effective methods of stress management, why not have the places where you recline or lie down be as comfortable as possible?

Creating comfort in your home means more than just filling it with material goods that enhance that comfort. Although that is certainly one viable way to make your home more cozy and secure, the quality of the relationships within your home is equal, if not more important, and either adds to the relaxation and comfort level or detracts from it.

To the extent that there is conflict, irritability, lack of intimacy, or lack of a sense of acceptance and security, there will be little psychological comfort no matter how soft your sofa is. So, increasing the comfort and reducing the stress in your home is both a physical, material issue and, more importantly, an emotional and psychological one.

Building comfort involves the creation of true psychological intimacy—defined as the degree to which you disclose yourself to another person. Home should be a safe place for everyone to share their innermost thoughts and feelings, including the fears, sense of vulnerability, anxiety, and even depression that remain these many months after September 11.

On the other hand, September 11 has spawned a renewed appreciation among many for the people they love the most and for their homes and families. This renewal has hopefully broken down some of the callousness with which many people before the tragedy of September 11 treated those who live closest to them, within their own homes and families.

In short, making home a safe and comfortable place means taking extra care with the people you love. Let them know often that you love them, and tell them the value they have in your life. Also, take care to treat everyone that lives or works under your roof with dignity and respect—your spouse, children, roommates, domestic employees, even pets.

Actions You Can Take to Enhance Your Comfort Zone

Define what *comfort* and *security* mean to you in emotional and psychological terms as well as in material terms. What can you do to make your home more comfortable, cozy, calming, and secure?

Here are some suggestions for feathering your nest and enhancing both your material and, more important, your emotional comfort at home.

- ◆ Buy some cozy blankets or throws for your bed or sofa; buy some new sheets for your bed; splurge on a super-soft down comforter and/or pillows.

- ◆ Gather your family members in the most comfortable place in your home and spend several minutes telling them, one by one, *specific* ways in which you appreciate them.

- Declare a "Home-Warming" day. Have everyone that lives with you contribute a gift that will add to the comfort of your home. Gifts or contributions can either be store-bought or made by loving hands. Be sure everyone participates, including kids.

- Establish a new habit of convening once-per-month house meetings. Use the time to identify and solve any problems that may be causing stress or conflict at home.

- Have a potluck Sunday night, old-fashioned dinner. Invite family and/or close friends and ask each guest to bring a favorite dish, preferably something that has been home-cooked.

- Rent some great old movies on video or DVD. Make some popcorn, cuddle up, and have a movie marathon.

- Fix, repair, replace, or clean up something that's been bothering you in your house or apartment.

- Pet your dog or cat an extra five minutes today.

- On the next cold night, gather round your fireplace, play background music, and read aloud short stories or a terrific novel. Or listen to a wonderful book on tape or to recordings of old-time radio shows.

- Have a game-night-at-home. Order some pizza and play cards, Monopoly, Scrabble, Trivial Pursuit, or other fun games.

CHAPTER 9

Step 6: Making Connections

"Out of the Rubble Comes a Need to Connect" was the headline of a November 25, 2001, story in the *Los Angeles Times*. The article pointed out what many of my colleagues have long known but not fully articulated until quite recently: "When we experience a big trauma like this [the events of September 11]," according to Harvard Medical School psychologist Nancy Etcoff, "the first impulse is to seek comfort. For human beings, the greatest source of well-being is love—between men and women, or mother and child.... We get the most pleasure from each other. In the face of tragedy, we want to return to powerful feelings of *connection* with other people." (Emphasis added.)

What did *you* do on September 11 and in the days and weeks that followed? Did you seek out a spouse or lover or parents or children or friends? And did they seek you out, too?

Did you connect? If not, did you *want* to connect but have no one to turn to?

The far-reaching impact of September 11 was not limited to those who were proximate or directly impacted upon by the attacks. Those who say that it was are wrong. And those who feel guilty or as though they have no right to feel emotional because they were hundreds or thousands of miles away at the time of the attack are troubling themselves unnecessarily by feeling guilty for having feelings.

"Many people who didn't know anyone killed in the attacks were touched. They have absorbed tragedy's residue like a nonsmoker taking in secondary smoke. They weren't close enough to inhale the most pungent fumes, but they've still been transformed," wrote Mimi Avins in the *Los Angeles Times* article cited above.

Avins goes on to highlight stories of couples who accelerated their wedding dates after the events of September 11. They had decided some time ago to get married, but before September 11 they were in a state of procrastination—thinking that they had plenty of time to make that commitment and walk down the aisle. But since September 11, people's thinking has changed and life decisions have taken on new urgency: *"Life is short. Every day is precious. If not now, when?"*

What's happening here is easy to understand and explain. Singles now feel that there is no time to waste—finding a life partner seems far more urgent than it did before September 11. Home and family have a stronger pull than ever before for many single or divorced people.

First Lady Laura Bush, speaking at a *Woman's Day* magazine awards luncheon in Manhattan on October 30, 2001, asserted, "Couples are coming together and staying together. Since September 11, divorce cases have been withdrawn at higher rates, and more people are buying engagement rings and planning weddings."

While Mrs. Bush's comments may be more wishful fancy than objective thinking (i.e., there are no census statistics or other data to confirm the trend she claims has occurred), they do seem to reflect our need for *meaningful* connections to others.

Consider how the events of September 11 have affected those in bad relationships and bad marriages, particularly those who have or had been "on the fence" about whether to stay or leave an existing relationship. September 11 has served as a needed catalyst for many who feel the need to become connected, but maybe not with the person they're currently with. September 11 has pushed them hard, either one way or the other.

The *Los Angeles Times* article above cited a local divorce attorney who noticed a flipped or reversed pattern among a score of men and women he had met with since September 11 who had been contemplating divorce. The lawyer's interpretation: "Women are more decisive. They want to get it over with and go on with their lives. Men are asking for a chance to make their marriages work. The funny thing is, before the attacks, the gender reactions were reversed."

There is nothing scientific about these observations. But, in my clinical experience, and in my observations of those afflicted by the September 11 Syndrome, both the quality and the quantity of relationships in people's lives have taken on greater urgency and importance. In other words, while people clearly feel the need to be connected, they also feel more strongly the need to be connected to the *right* person.

Avins makes the point that "'Who you gonna call?' used to mean something else. Two months into the scary world that terrorism has wrought, the question isn't just the goofy refrain of the Ghostbusters' anthem. It's the measure of isolation. Who would care if your plane crashed? Who would tell Katie Couric, with conviction, that you'd enriched their lives?"

Much of the lingering depression associated with the September 11 Syndrome derives from a sense of loss. We feel it through empathy and compassion for those whose loved ones were lost in the tragedies on that day, as well as through the anticipation of loss of those we love and hold dear. Such anticipated loss is best countered by focusing on the preciousness of the connections and people that fill your life now, rather than on the precariousness of life and the inevitability of eventual loss of loved ones through aging, illness, accident, or attack.

Whenever a major event brings the tenuousness of life into clear focus, people respond by seeking connection. Doing so is a potent and adaptive stress reducer—provided that the relationships are not dysfunctional or marred or contaminated by destructive, futile conflict. Universally, for people who are single, divorced, or widowed, the quest of seeking and affirming connections involves looking with greater purpose for meaningful, committed relationships.

Connection also involves affirming or reaffirming important family ties—with both nuclear families and extended families. After September 11, major family holidays like Thanksgiving, Christmas, Chanukah, and Ramadan are far more meaningful and poignant for many.

It is not at all unusual in many homes to observe the Thanksgiving ritual of going around the table to say what you are thankful for. But at the first Thanksgiving after September 11, prayers of sympathy and consolation for the victims and their families could be heard nationwide alongside expressions of thanks to be together as a family. The impact of September 11, which was felt all over the country, seemed to give new meaning to the word *thanksgiving*—almost as though many were hearing and appreciating the word for the first time.

Connection is also often sought and affirmed by seeking a closer relationship with God, or a spiritual power, and a greater sense of community with the congregations of religious groups. That this connection is sought is important because studies in health psychology have repeatedly shown the stress reduction and health-enhancing effects of spiritual beliefs and of involvement and connection with fellow congregants.

Other obvious connections have been made through a tremendous upsurge in charitable giving, blood donations, volunteer work, and a myriad of other ways.

As others have pointed out, whatever the terrorists hoped to accomplish by their despicable actions, just the opposite has occurred. If they thought their plot would drive us apart as a nation, they couldn't have been more wrong. We are stronger and more united than ever.

The new patriotism we feel, which has become so much a part of the New Normalcy, represents successful connections in ways not seen since World War II.

We feel more connected to one another as an American people when we collectively and proudly display the symbols of our patriotism and heritage of freedom. Having a common enemy—the "evildoers" or terrorists—bonds us together as Americans and, indeed, increases our sense of connection with long-standing allies (such as Great Britain) who have stood shoulder-to-shoulder with us in the coalition against terror. That alliance is reminiscent of the way America supported Great Britain in her hour of greatest need during the darkest days of World War II.

Even Democrats and Republicans, in a virtually unprecedented display of bipartisanship, reached out across the aisle to support the country and the president with one voice. This ethos of bipartisanship in American politics—at least as it pertains to the prosecution of the war on terrorism—is another form of connection. We have the sense that more unites us than divides us on partisan political lines, especially when the full United States Senate stood hand in hand on the steps of the U.S. Capitol and sang "God Bless America" just a day or so after September 11.

Actions You Can Take to Seek and Affirm Connections

Here are some things you can do to help make or strengthen your own connections:

◆ Think about and affirm your values regarding interpersonal, familial, spiritual, and patriotic connections in your life.

- Tell the people you love that you love them—on a regular basis. No one can hear that said too often, especially children.

- Express and receive physical affection; make love better and more often.

- Call some old friends and reconnect.

- Call your extended family.

- Host or participate in family gatherings and in reunions; be a driving force in getting your family together.

- Affirm your spiritual connections—with both people and with God; pray.

- Feel connected to fellow Americans because of the values that define us and the freedoms we are fighting to protect and defend.

- Take pride in the American military.

- Volunteer in your community.

- Take comfort in your strongest and most powerful connections with other people; take the time to nurture those connections.

- Replace thoughts and fears of loss of those most important to you with thoughts of gratitude and appreciation of the time you have to share with them.

- If September 11 has made you more acutely aware of your loneliness and the absence of meaningful, committed relationships, take renewed action and set your intention to find and develop your desired commitment and/or relationship. For example, a 39-year-old divorced woman quoted in the Avins article says she has resolved not to date men who don't share her goals. "Something's permanently shifted for me. All I've been thinking about lately is finding the right person, who wants the same things I do— to have a home and a family. Even with friends, I'm much pickier about whom I spend time with now. Everything seems more urgent."

◆ Work on improving the quality of relationships you currently have; seek professional help if conflict is unresolved and recurrent or if your relationships are not as satisfying or fulfilling as you desire.

Finding Love Among the Ruins

Seeking and affirming connections with spouses, children, families, lovers, extended family, friends, God, community, and country, as a by-product of September 11, are powerful stress-reducers and potent ways for us to actually *thrive*, even under the riskier, more uncertain times that define the New Normalcy.

"There is something life-affirming about discovering love, or longing for it, among the ruins," concluded Avins.

CHAPTER 10

Step 7: Finding Your Personal Courage

Amer), merica's response to the events of September 11 demonstrated to the world the depth of our people's resolve, heroism, generosity, and personal courage.

But what is personal courage? And how can struggling to find your own meaning of personal courage help move you beyond merely coping to an optimal level of *thriving* in these risky and uncertain times? In this chapter, we'll discuss techniques to identify and strengthen your own personal courage. You'll learn how finding your well of personal courage lets you exercise some measure of control over your life again.

Defining Personal Courage

Many people misunderstand or misconstrue the concept of *courage*. For example, they may think of it solely in terms of physical bravery or derring-do, such as that displayed by the heroic passengers on Flight 93 who challenged the hijackers and crashed the plane into an empty field in Pennsylvania. Or, they may describe the noble, selfless attempts of rescue workers who charged *up* the World Trade Center stairwells—seemingly without fear for their own lives—to help innocent civilians run *down* and away from the towering, imploding infernos.

Like many others, you may even believe that courageous people don't experience the same fears, anxiety, sense of helplessness, or self-doubts with which you may occasionally or frequently struggle. Nothing could be farther from the truth.

Courageous people do not perform heroically because they *lack* fear. On the contrary, their heroism and courage lie in their ability to meet fear and anxiety head-on, and to act *in spite of* the fact that they may be frightened nearly out of their wits.

Moving Forward in the Face of Fear

By definition, courage means moving forward *in the face of fear*. Think about it: Without the presence of fear and anxiety, the concept of courage would be meaningless or, at minimum, unnecessary.

Finding and flexing your personal courage will help protect your health—both physical and emotional—from the ravaging negative effects of stress. We know that people with stress-resistant personalities *thrive* in risky times because they find the resolve to act even though they may be mightily afraid and deeply uncertain about what today—let alone tomorrow—might bring.

You may recall from Chapter 3 that the ability to thrive under stress derives from three core qualities of character—the three Cs or secrets of psychological hardiness: control, challenge, and commitment.

Using these superb life-preserving coping skills, hardy personalities can turn great adversities into opportunities. As fabled industrialist Henry Kaiser once said, "I always view problems as opportunities in work clothes."

In my view, out of the horrors of September 11, a new, expanded definition of psychological hardiness and stress resistance has begun to take shape. If we choose to unearth and cleanse them, precious psychological gifts may be discovered amidst the rubble and carnage of September 11. But, *make no mistake*, this date, too, shall live in infamy as a colossal display of man's capacity to do evil. In a safe and sane world, the horrific events of that fateful day should never have happened. Yet, they did occur and our challenge now—as a nation and as individuals—is to turn that adversity into opportunities for meaning and transformation.

As the fog of our collective trauma clears, we can see the outline of new and perhaps even more valuable life lessons in how to cope and to thrive in times of terrorism, unnamed risk, and seemingly boundless uncertainty.

These new lessons in stress resistance are embodied in three post-September 11 secrets of psychological hardiness. These additional Cs are *comfort* and *connection*, which we discussed in the last two chapters, and now, at a deeply individual level—your own personal *courage*.

Terrorists win, after all, when they frighten us so much and make our lives so unpredictable and terrifying that we inhibit our own actions, fearing the consequences of exercising our personal and collective freedoms. In this sense, personal courage is the antidote to avoidance.

Consider the personal courage reflected in the response of Israeli political theorist Yaron Ezrahi as told to columnist Thomas L. Friedman of *The New York Times*: "Every time I walk in Jerusalem I know that a car might blow up next to me. But I still go out, because life without affirmation is no life at all."

Being courageous doesn't require that you take unnecessary and unacceptable risks. But it does mean making informed choices about where you will go and what you will—and will not—do. The important point here is that the choices are *yours*; they are not choices dictated by some terrorist organization half a world away, or even half a block away.

Long before the events of September 11, we all faced a number of risks each day, from natural disasters to accidents in cars, trains, planes, and buses; from crime to homegrown terrorism—such as the bombing in Oklahoma City or school shooters at schools around the country. In California, where I live, there is a risk that each day may bring the "big one"—the killer quake on the San Andreas fault line, which traverses the state, or any of its smaller derivative fault lines.

Today, my daughter does school drills on earthquake preparedness. But those of us who lived through the Cold War era grew up doing "drop drills," in which we were sharply reminded of the ever-present anxiety that an atomic bomb would be dropped or a nuclear missile launched at the United States.

Although the particulars change over time, we still must always deal with some form of danger, and while the risks we now face are indeed ominous, evil, and destructive, they are new only in content, not in form. By this I mean that we have coped with, and in some cases overcome, other perilous threats and risks of global ruin by finding and flexing the personal courage that lies deep within each of us.

While we have directed our courage toward different, more familiar *types* of risk, it has always been—and remains today—our personal courage that allows us to move forward through the fear, to live and even thrive in the face of what have always been the ever-present dangers inherent in daily life.

So, how *did* we find the courage to cope with these risks that were with us long before September 11? And, more important, how do we ensure that our courage doesn't fail us now so that we can cope and, indeed, even thrive in the aftermath of those terrifying events?

Perhaps without realizing it, you have probably already been using at least one potent defense mechanism long before September 11 to deal with the risks and fears of daily life. That defense mechanism is *denial*. That's right: a psychologist is telling you to go ahead and use denial—provided you do so in ways that improve rather than constrain the quality of your life. When used effectively to control anxiety without disturbing or disrupting your other life functioning, denial is a useful coping skill more correctly labeled as *adaptive denial*.

Using Adaptive Denial

Adaptive denial is the ability to assert to yourself that you *will* go forward in the face of fear and anxiety with the capacity to put the frightening thoughts out of your mind. It depends on your making the assertion that "It (the dreaded event) simply won't happen to me or won't happen here or won't happen today." Or "If there is nothing that I can do to control this, I have to just keep on living my life banking on faith (and denial)."

If you let the fear, anxiety, and depression spawned by the cataclysmic events of September 11 alter your mobility, your ability to conduct your daily life, and your capacity to experience joy as well as entertainment and other means of much-needed distraction, then the terrorists win. And they defeat *you* at a deeply personal level.

Making Informed Choices

Coping does not have to depend solely on adaptive denial. That's just a good start. Defining the limits of your personal courage also means taking a careful assessment and inventory of your life. In this way, mustering your courage involves using your intellectual ability to collect information in order to calculate *relative risks*. In other words, using the information available to you and your own value system, you must decide which risks are minimal, tolerable, worth it, or just too great. And then, act accordingly.

So what risks do you face in going about your daily life? What can you do to prepare for those risks or to minimize the likelihood of their occurrence? What is in your control, and what is not?

You will need to become explicit about what you will choose to do, even in the face of risk, anxiety, and fear. If you avoid making these hard choices—which you are "free" to do—you will, paradoxically, sacrifice or, at minimum, compromise your freedom. Exercising free choice, after all, is both the benefit and the responsibility of being a free people.

Defining the limits of your personal courage also requires you to be explicit about what you will *not* choose to do. There may be some risks or fears that are too strong for you to tolerate or too great, in your estimation, to make a particular activity worth doing.

Remember that even if it were possible, there is a tremendously high price attached to avoiding all risk and danger as a way to cope with anxiety and fear. If you allow anxiety and fear to control your life, you will likely spend a great deal of time engaged in avoidance activities.

For example, people with agoraphobia have an irrational fear of going outside away from their "comfort zones." To avoid the panic and anxiety they feel when they leave the security of their own homes, they stay indoors, becoming prisoners of their own fears. Clearly, they become victims of their avoidance strategies. Most of us would agree that when the price of avoidance is so high that it interrupts your ability to work, socialize, go to school, or to take care of your daily life requirements, the cost is simply too great.

Guarding the principle of freedom on the home front requires you to make risk choices and to take personal responsibility for your actions and for their consequences. When you have chosen to assume informed risks *and* taken action to move ahead in their wake, you will have demonstrated important aspects of your personal courage.

Staying "Vigilant"

Defining the limits of your personal courage also requires understanding what it means for you to be vigilant. First, it is imperative to distinguish between the concept of *vigilance*, which means enhanced awareness, and *hypervigilance*, which is a maladaptive, dysfunctional state of alarm and panic. In the current circumstances, vigilance is desirable and adaptive; hypervigilance is not.

As a coping response to heightened danger and risk, vigilance can be life-preserving. By developing greater awareness of and sensitivity to your surroundings, by becoming more vigilant to unusual behavior in others or to deviations from expected or usual circumstances, you will become better prepared and less vulnerable to danger.

Developing vigilance requires an appreciation of the relationship between stress, or arousal, and the quality or ability to think and to act adaptively. Psychological research shows that optimal performance is best achieved at medium or moderate levels of physiological and cognitive arousal. In other words, being *too* relaxed lowers your guard, increases vulnerability to risk, and reduces performance quality including your ability to detect, escape, or avoid danger.

Likewise, being overly "amped up" or "hyper" impairs your judgment, produces impulsive action and fragmented thinking, induces panic, and reduces overall performance quality in other ways, thereby heightening vulnerability to danger.

The bottom line: Contrary to the admonishments of Homeland Security Director Tom Ridge, vigilance is best attained through a *moderate* rather than through a *high* state of alert.

Maintaining adaptive vigilance also requires that you have a basic action plan should your newly sensitized psychological radar pick up on signs or signals of what you deem to be a "credible" threat or perception of danger. Ask yourself what kind of suspicious behavior in others or unusual circumstances you might observe if your awareness dial was properly tuned to vigilance. What would you do with that information? Who would you call to report it? What could you do to protect yourself and others should the need arise?

When you are vigilant as opposed to panicky, you also are better able to utilize critical internal signals to detect danger and to accurately assess a situation. Long before high technology and the Information Age, the psychoanalyst Carl Jung wrote that knowledge is available to each of us from at least four of our own established internal channels: *thinking, intuiting, sensing,* and *feeling.*

When you are truly vigilant, you become very aware of the cues and clues in your external environment. But the meaning or significance of that information is then available to you to interpret by using input from your own built-in "multimodal processing" system: your ability to think, feel, and sense and to use your intuition. It's all there: You merely need to tune into the appropriate channels of knowledge.

A word of caution: Beware of staying vigilant for too long without periods of relaxation, rest, and restorative sleep. Overactivation of the vigilance response can produce fatigue, panic, and distortions in information processing. Director Ridge has offered the terminology "alert fatigue" to describe the risks of prolonged states of vigilance that can deteriorate into hypervigilance.

In worst cases, hypervigilance can lead to full-blown panic attacks and even paranoid thinking. Remember, hypervigilance and panic do not lower your vulnerability to risk and danger; they greatly increase it.

So, be sure to "stand down" periodically from a stance of vigilance. As a rule of thumb, your own state of vigilance shouldn't extend beyond four hours at a stretch. And even that stretch should be punctuated by regular "time outs" or relaxation breaks ideally of 10 to 20 minutes. Using the relaxation and mind excursion techniques you have already learned can give you optimal benefits from even short relaxation breaks and will help prevent hypervigilance from developing.

And you absolutely *must* sleep. Hypervigilance plus sleep deprivation is a formula for disaster, *not* personal courage.

Your Personal Courage

If your courage has sometimes or even often failed you since September 11, you're certainly not alone. Rest assured: Finding it again won't be as difficult as you might think.

Keep in mind that the word *personal* in this context means that it is *your* definition of courage that matters. Don't try to live up to what you think others expect of you or to perform up to someone else's definition or standards. Remember, too, that courage involves feeling anxiety, experiencing fear, and moving forward anyway *in spite of* those very difficult emotions.

While you probably haven't noticed, you've been exercising personal courage all along by the mere fact of living each day with absolutely no firm guarantees of what tomorrow will bring. It has always required personal courage to live with the risks you can name or imagine. Now you are challenged to live even more fully because the once unimaginable has become a hard, ugly, and fully imagined reality.

The methods you learned in the preceding chapters will aid you in finding your personal courage. Embracing these techniques will help you gain control of anxiety that is stimulated by disturbing negative thoughts and images. Calming yourself with relaxation exercises and techniques will allow your courage to reappear unimpeded by crippling doubt and paralyzing fear and anxiety.

If the appeal of rational argument works for you, use it: Talk yourself out of freezing from fear by looking at the data. For example, you know that the relative risk of having a car accident is far greater than of something happening on a plane, whether it is caused by accident or by a terrorist act.

Or think about this: Terrorists specialize in *surprise* attacks. Unpredictability is the calling card of terrorism. So, the very things that we worry about and fear— because they have already happened—are actually unlikely to happen again precisely because the surprise factor won't be there.

Take comfort, too, in the fact that while our government, intelligence, and law enforcement agencies were far too lax on September 10, they are now professional worriers on high alert today. (Because they are professionals, learning to control hypervigilance and panic even while on high alert is part of their program.) Even while you sleep, these "good guys" are thinking about all the "what if" scenarios and making plans for your protection. Since they are the ones primarily in control, as long as they're worried, perhaps you don't have to be.

In fact, mere days after September 11, FBI Director Robert Mueller announced that the Bureau was redeploying its agents so that 75 percent of them would devote themselves full time to counterterrorism measures.

So your personal courage should be bolstered by the knowledge that Americans have tremendous government resources on the job of anticipating and hopefully preventing another major terrorist attack. Right now, as our military and intelligence strategists are thinking up "worst case" scenarios and planning for them, your personal courage enjoys what Pentagon types call a tremendous "force multiplier." In other words, the power and courage of "one"—that is, of you—is multiplied and extended by the resources of American might and mind, brains, and brawn.

Remind yourself that each time you can muster your will to move forward, to go and do what you have feared or avoided previously, your personal courage will become stronger. Whether this means flying on a plane, or traveling across a bridge or through a tunnel; attending a concert or a sporting event, or going to a mall, or in an elevator in a high-rise building, your success in living courageously will be emboldened. When you successfully accomplish any fearful act, you will be fighting against terrorism in your own way, in a meaningful way, by moving forward in the face of fear.

With each success, your anxiety will decrease while the scope of your world and the space within which you are free to move, widen.

We all have a choice to live in a closed society constrained by our individual and collective fears, or in a free society, terrorists be damned. In a real sense, how each of us defines and then exercises our personal courage will determine which society we are choosing to create or preserve.

Writing in *The New York Times*, Thomas Friedman defined a closed society as one that is "based not on freedom and trust but on fear and mistrust. This would probably wipe out terrorism, but it would be an awful place to live. The other option is to accept slightly less freedom, tolerate a little less trust, and continue living in a basically open society—but accept that there will be terrorism in the cracks."

An open society is not for the fainthearted. It takes courage—personally and jointly—to protect freedom, the bedrock of our nation and our calling card in the world. "The culture of freedom and openness is not for softies," Friedman wrote in his column. He then added, "I'd rather steel myself to live in an open society with greater risks than live in a steel cage."

You do have a choice, and exercising your personal courage will help you to make it. If becoming more conscious of the risks inherent in an open society means forfeiting a little freedom in order to add a lot more vigilance, then that is a price we should all be prepared to pay.

A Final Thought:
Remember September 11

T he attack on Pearl Harbor happened more than sixty years ago. Yet the events are still recalled vividly. Older Americans remember where they were when they first heard the terrible news, and they can still think of how they felt when the reality of the attack and the loss of lives sank in. The next day, the United States went to war.

If we—even those of us who were born after 1941— can still conjure up deep emotions and empathy about Pearl Harbor more than six decades later, why should any of us believe the scars from the September 11 attacks would heal any sooner? They won't; moreover, they shouldn't.

It is wholly appropriate to feel sadness and mourn for the victims and their families, especially their children. And it is wholly fitting to remember the events of September 11 as a way to honor the memories of so many who lost their lives.

So, do not take from this book the idea that some of the "thought stopping" techniques discussed are intended to blot out all memories of that day. Remembering the day is well and good. It is just when thoughts of the attacks overwhelm you that it is appropriate to use any or all of the seven steps to help you "get a grip" and "return to normal."

At the same time, we must steel ourselves for the possibility—some say inevitability—that another attack may come. We all pray that never happens, certainly, but if it does and you find yourself in a more current version of the September 11 Syndrome, use these seven steps again and quickly.

Like Pearl Harbor, the September 11 attack will be in our minds forever. Like Pearl Harbor, let's honor the victims by remembering the event. And like Pearl Harbor, let us teach our children by showing them how Americans can rebound from adversity and thrive in challenging times.

Index

Behavioral antidepressants,
114–116
Benign denial, 14
Bio-terrorism. *See* Anthrax
Blood donation
terrorism and, 135
Breathing
relaxation, 102–103
Bush, George, 26, 28, 61
Bush, Laura, 133

C
Cardiovascular problems
as stress-related symptoms, 46
Central Intelligence Agency (CIA)
Tenet, George and, 2
Challenger space shuttle
explosion of, 67
Change, external
adapting to, 19
Charitable act
depression-incompatible
behavior and, 117–118, 135
Children
exposure to images and, 81–82
Choices
making informed, 144–145
Chronic stress, 45–53
acceptance and endurance of,
36–37
City of Hope Hospital, 119
Comfort zone, 6
creation of, 123–129
enhancement of, 128–129
Computer games
controlling negative thoughts
with, 88
Concentration
increase in stress, fear, anxiety
and, 48
Concerts
avoidance of, 49
Connections
making, 131–138

Connections *(continued)*
seeking and affirmation of,
136–138
Control, loss of
low-grade depression and, 51
Coping
with distress, 57–58, 143
effectively, 53, 58
psychological terms of, 57–58
Cotter, Holland, 24
Courage, personal, 148–151
definition of, 140
finding, 139–151
limits of, 144–145
Crossword puzzles
controlling negative thoughts
with, 88
Crowds
avoidance of, 49

D
Decision making, 96–98
increase in stress, fear, anxiety
and, 48
Democrats and Republicans, 136
Denial
adaptive, 143, 144
benign, 14
Department of Health. *See* New
York City Department of
Heath
Depersonalization, 42–43
Depression, 2, 50–51
morbid thinking and, 51
overcoming, 111–121
Depression incompatible
behaviors (DIBs), 114–115
activity and, 116–117
being helpful and, 117–118
charitable acts and, 117–118
cleaning house and, 119–120
entertainment and, 118–119
laughter and, 118–119
physical exercise and, 116–117

Stop-sign visualization exercise,
76–77, 87
Stress, 46
  chronic, 45–53
  fear, anxiety and, 47–48
  health and, 46, 48, 49, 58–59
  symptoms of, 46
  thriving under, 59–61
Stress, acute
  reactions, 41–45
  signs of, 42–44
  symptoms of, 38–39, 43
Stress disorder, posttraumatic
  (PTSD), 32, 34–35

T

Tanzania
  U.S. embassy in, 10
Tenet, George
  head of CIA, 2
Terrorism
  acute stress reaction and, 4
  after September 11, 12–13, 50,
    52–53
  alcoholism and, 45
  blood donation and, 135
  changes of life and, 13–15
  coping with, 2, 5, 14, 23, 26,
    28, 52–53, 143
  definition of, 26, 49
  degree of impact from, 25
  emotional difficulties with, 3,
    69–70
  emotional impact management
    of, 40–41
  footage of, 4–5
  on foreign soil, 10–12
  gaining control over, 23
  images of, 24
  indirect victims of, 35
  internal psychological defense
    mechanisms and, 15
  Internet and, 32
  isolation and, 3–4

Terrorism (*continued*)
  making connections after,
    131–138
  marriages and, 133
  mind changes and, 15–24
  national psyche affected by, 17
  perception of risk and,
    24–27
  polls on, 2, 25
  positive side of, 61
  prejudices and, 47
  prescription drugs and, 45
  probability of, 24–25
  public mentioning of, 1
  relationships and, 133
  responding to, 27–29
  sense of cause with, 134
  before September 11, 10–12
  stress of, 1
  threat of, 39
  trauma of, 34, 40
  understanding, 31–53
  volunteer work and, 125
Theaters
  avoidance of, 49
"Thought Stopping," 5, 154
Thoughts, negative, 71–72
  chronic indecisiveness and,
    96–98
  controlling of, 85–98
  decision making and, 96–98
  diversion of, 88–89
  fears and, 90–94
  fighting of, 72–75
  geography game and, 89
  limiting exposure of, 95–96
  math countdown and, 90
  mental distraction of, 88–89
  rubber-band snap and,
    87–88
  techniques for stopping of,
    87–88
Thriving in uncertain times,
  58–62, 139

About the Author

Bestselling author Dr. Harriet Braiker has been a practicing clinical psychologist and management consultant in Los Angeles and management consultant in Los Angeles for more than 25 years. The author of several highly successful popular psychology books, she is also a much sought-after speaker, especially to women's groups and corporations, on a wide range of topics. She has been a contributing editor and columnist for *Working Woman* and *Lear's*, and has also written for many other national women's magazines. In addition, she is the award-winning author of numerous research books and other publications. Dr. Braiker has appeared many times on such national talk shows as *Oprah, The Today Show, Larry King, Live with Regis and Kathy Lee, Hour Magazine, Sonya Live,* the NBC *Nightly News with Tom Brokaw,* and CNN.